# IMPERIAL St. PETERSBURG

*Pages from History*

1 7 0 3 ◆ 1 9 1 7

*Based on Material
from the State Museum
of the History
of St. Petersburg*

PAINTINGS

PRINTS AND DRAWINGS

SCULPTURE

APPLIED ART

EVERYDAY OBJECTS

POSTERS

PORCELAIN AND GLASS

Art Lux
АРТ-ЛЮКС

Foreword by Natalia Dementyeva

Selection by Alla Povelikhina

Text by Olga Chekanova, Galina Urusova,
Georgy Priamursky and Irina Silantyeva

Notes by Galina Vasilyeva, Albina Pavelkina,
Konstantin Zhetarchuk (Paintings, Prints and Drawings)
Liudmila Aksenova (Applied Arts, Everyday Objects)
Elena Korzhevskaya (Popular Prints, Posters etc.)
Tatyana Kumzerova (Porcelain and Glass)

General supervision by Boris Kirikov

Translated from the Russian by Paul Williams, Yuri Pamfilov,
Jennifer Cahn and Maria Zavialova

Layout and design by Andrei Novozhilov

Photographs by Alexander Kashnitsky

---

FRONT COVER ILLUSTRATION:

*Parade in front of the Winter Palace*
*First quarter of the 19th century*
*Engraving tinted with watercolor*
*44 x 68*

ON PAGE 6:

*Symbolic key to the city of St. Petersburg*
*with the monogram of Catherine II.*
*1780s*
*Ormolu. Contained in a case. 27 x 11*

* ALL MEASUREMENTS ARE IN CENTIMETERS

ISBN 5-900293-03-3     ART-LUX. St.Petersburg     Gummerus Printing 1996

# Contents

*Natalia Dementyeva.*
FOREWORD
—— 5 ——

*Olga Chekanova.*
THE FOUNDING AND BUILDING OF THE NEW
RUSSIAN CAPITAL, ST.PETERSBURG. 1703–1917
—— 7 ——

*Galina Urusova.*
EMPEROR PETER I, THE GREAT
—— 13 ——

*Galina Urusova.*
EMPRESS ANNA I IOANNOVNA
—— 27 ——

*Galina Urusova.*
EMPRESS ELIZABETH
—— 35 ——

*Galina Urusova.*
EMPRESS CATHERINE II, THE GREAT
—— 49 ——

*Galina Urusova.*
EMPEROR PAUL I
—— 67 ——

*Olga Chekanova.*
EMPEROR ALEXANDER I
—— 75 ——

*Olga Chekanova.*
EMPEROR NICHOLAS I
—— 93 ——

*Olga Chekanova.*
EMPEROR ALEXANDER II
——113——

*Georgy Priamursky.*
EMPEROR ALEXANDER III
——125——

*Georgy Priamursky.*
EMPEROR NICHOLAS II
——135——

*Irina Silantyeva.*
APPENDIX.
BIOGRAPHIES OF THE EMPERORS
——155——

# FOREWORD

The present edition traces the history of St. Petersburg through all the stages of its development as the capital of Russia from its foundation in 1703 until the October Revolution of 1917, the year after which the capital was transferred to Moscow.

St. Petersburg arose on the shores of the Baltic as the advance post of sweeping transformations carried out by Peter the Great in the eighteenth century. Founded as a military fortress, it became the capital of Russia in 1712 and developed into a cultural and scientific center of world significance.

During the eighteenth and nineteenth centuries the city was built according to a single, well-thought-out plan by such outstanding architects as Andreas Schlüter, Domenico Trezzini, Francesco Bartolomeo Rastrelli, Giacomo Quarenghi, Antonio Rinaldi, Adrian Zakharov, Andrei Voronikhin, Carlo Rossi and Auguste Montferrand, to name but a few.

The historical center of St. Petersburg, its granite-clad embankments and the Neva River are famous for their striking beauty which never fails to captivate visitors, causing many of them to return again and again. No wonder that in 1990 UNESCO listed the city center and the architectural complexes in the suburbs among the key world heritage sights.

The edition *Imperial St. Petersburg* has been prepared by researchers of the State Museum of the History of St. Petersburg (The Peter and Paul Fortress), the museum with the longest history in the city. Its stocks totalling nearly 1,000,000 items (paintings, prints and drawings, objects of decorative and applied art, everyday articles, and many other things) shed light on various aspects of life in St. Petersburg.

Natalia Dementyeva
Director of the Museum

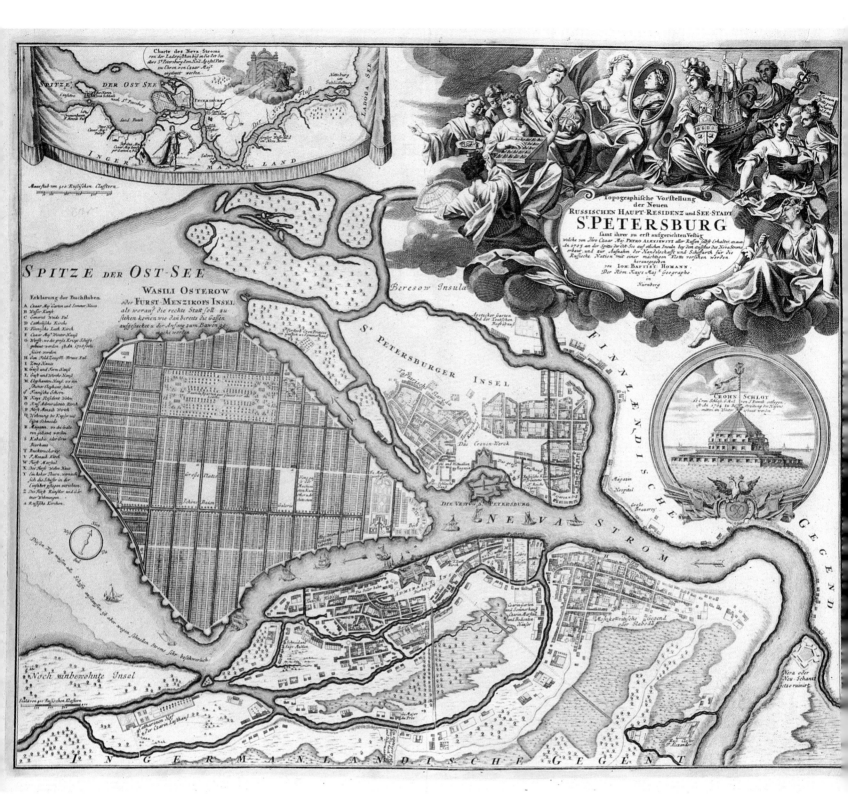

PLAN OF ST. PETERSBURG

*1720s*
*Published by Johann Baptista Homann*
*49.5 x 58.5*

*This is one of the earliest plans of St. Petersburg. In the upper left is the Neva River which flows from Lake Ladoga to the Gulf of Finland. On the right are allegories of the arts and sciences and a portrait of Emperor Peter I. In the circle is the Kronslot Fortress on the Gulf. The plan shows the Peter and Paul Fortress, the Admiralty Fortress, and construction on Petersburg Island and the Neva's left bank. The clear-cut layout of Vasilyevsky Island, surrounded by fortress structures, is presented following the draft of the architect Domenico Trezzini approved by Peter I in 1716.*

# THE FOUNDING AND BUILDING OF THE NEW RUSSIAN CAPITAL, ST. PETERSBURG

## *(1703 – 1917)*

St. Petersburg is a city which lies by the sea, but its character is not entirely defined by its proximity to the Gulf of Finland. The city's layout depends to a great extent on the Neva River with its branches and numerous canals. Situated in the Neva delta, St. Petersburg spreads over many islands, the largest of which – Admiralteisky, Vasilyevsky and Gorodovoi (the Petrograd Side) – are part of the downtown area. In the early twentieth century there were 101 islands and despite the fact that their number has decreased by half, the city has not lost its distinctive character, determined by the high level of rivers and canals, and the low level of land on which it is built. Its uniqueness also springs from the fact that the waterways reflect the city's layout, landscape and general atmosphere more vividly than the streets. Thanks to the water, the architectural aspect of the city possesses something special that the visitor will not see anywhere else. The Neva River plays an extremely important role in the layout of the city, being the main "prospekt" of St. Petersburg. Overlooking the Neva are the buildings of the Admiralty and the palaces that line the granite embankments. Almost in the middle of the river, on an island, rise the walls of the Peter and Paul Fortress and the golden spire of the Peter and Paul Cathedral (122.5 m high). The gilt dome of St. Isaac's Cathedral is visible from far out in the Gulf.

The city, located on islands, naturally has many bridges. Their number is never fixed. For different reasons some bridges are built, others disappear, but by the beginning of the twentieth century there were around 800 bridges. The granite embankments and the fine ironwork of the bridges beautifully complement the pale blueness of the sky and the unruffled surface of rivers and canals. However, the waters here are not always calm. Floods occur quite often in St. Petersburg, caused by strong Atlantic cyclones over the Baltic. Almost every year in late fall, when strong westerly winds drive heavy waves into the Gulf, the water level in the Neva rises and sometimes the river overflows its banks, flooding the nearby streets and squares.

Founded by Peter I, St. Petersburg was not the only settlement on the Neva banks at that time. Further up the river there was a Swedish fortress, Nyenskans, which had received the status of a town in 1632 and which the Swedes had considered rebuilding. But after the defeat of Sweden in the Great Northern War and the founding of St. Petersburg the fort was destroyed and its site later became part of the city. Building his new capital Peter I was guided by the latest European achievements in town planning and fortification. Traditionally in Old Russia towns had developed haphazardly. Therefore for the implementation of his new concept of a regularly laid out city Peter needed the experience of foreign specialists. With this in mind he invited a large number of Western European architects, engineers and garden designers to Russia.

The city grew up around the St. Petersburg Fortress, built on a small island in the mouth of the Neva, spreading east to Gorodovoi Island just outside the fortress. Here the first harbor was built, not far from Trinity Square, named after the wooden Church of the Holy Trinity, in 1703. The biggest structure in the city was a Gostiny Dvor storehouse. On the opposite bank of the Neva, construction of the first shipyard, the Admiralty, was started. The first stone buildings began to spring up along the banks of the Neva and its main branch, the Malaya Nevka, including the palace of Peter himself.

Unlike many other cities that developed gradually, in pace with the economic development of the country, St. Petersburg grew with unprecedented speed, being the result of intensive and purposeful planning. Peter I was not only the founder of the city, he also conceived the first building schemes and expressed the idea of making Vasilyevsky Island the center of the city. The reali-

zation of this concept began in 1712 after the capital of Russia was transferred from Moscow to St. Petersburg.

Construction on Vasilyevsky Island started in 1716 according to the general plan worked out by the Swiss-born architect Domenico Trezzini. He was the first and chief architect of the capital. He supervised the construction of the St. Petersburg fortress and made drafts for the general plan of the city and "model" private houses to suit different classes of society. According to this plan, the Spit of Vasilyevsky Island was to become the administrative and commercial center of the city with a large square flanked by government buildings and trading quarters.

This project, however, did not quite satisfy Peter I. Construction was already in progress, but he was still thinking of another, more perfect, plan, and on February 8, 1717 a new "general draft of St. Petersburg" was submitted for his approval. It was presented by the outstanding French architect Jean-Baptiste Le Blond who had come to Russia on Peter's invitation. This project embodied the most advanced ideas of contemporary town planning that found expression in the use of layout methods characteristic of "ideal" towns in Western Europe but not quite suitable for local conditions. For this reason construction of St. Petersburg continued according to the general plan of Trezzini that proved to be more realistic, although it was also based on principles of regular layout.

The project for the development of Vasilyevsky Island was not carried out in full but a memory of it still survives in the layout of the island which resembles a rectangular grid of parallel streets and intersecting "perspectives," making the area a unique monument of "regular" town planning. Peter's idea of creating the city for center here was not realized either. All major buildings began to appear along the opposite bank of the Neva, on the Admiralty Side, where the future city center gradually came into its own with

Nevsky Prospekt as the main street.

In 1737, to regulate construction activity in the city and finally resolve the problem of its center, a Commission for the Construction of St. Petersburg was established. For four years the architectural department of this committee, headed by Pyotr Eropkin, worked out plans for the improvement of the populated areas and the development of new districts.

In the 1730s, reconstruction of the old Admiralty building began. According to the new general plan, it was to become the dominant architectural feature in a system of three central thoroughfares: Nevsky Prospekt, Voznesensky Prospekt and Gorokhovaya Street, intersected by the Moika and Fontanka Rivers and the Catherine Canal. The golden spire of the Admiralty became the key point in the St. Petersburg skyline.

Many buildings, such as the *Kunstkammer* (Cabinet of Curios) and the Twelve *Collegia*, or Colleges (Ministries), begun under Peter I, were completed in the reign of Anna I, which was relatively long and saw intensive construction. The designs of these buildings incorporated elements of the Baroque style which flourished in St. Petersburg in the time of Elizabeth, daughter of Peter I, in the middle of the eighteenth century. This lavish style was most evident in the Winter Palace, the principal imperial residence built in the 1750s by the great Italian-born architect Francesco Bartolomeo Rastrelli, who skillfully combined Western European and Russian traditions in his creations.

The reign of Elizabeth was marked by the revival of the national Russian tradition of building five-domed churches. This tradition went back to ancient times and was interrupted in the Petrine era by the introduction of basilica-like single-spire churches. The Baroque period culminated in the creation of magnificent royal residences at Peterhof, Tsarskoye Selo and Strelna, all designed by Rastrelli.

In the 1760s, the Baroque gave way to Classicism, a style that sought to inculcate the antique ideals of "noble simplicity and serene grandeur." The appearance of Classicism is associated with the reign of Catherine II who entertained the ideas of the Enlightenment in the spheres of politics, philosophy and art, architecture in particular. Her attitudes left their stamp on all facets of contemporary life and greatly influenced the development of St. Petersburg.

As the Empress herself put it, she was seized with a passion for building. This passion manifested itself in the construction of numerous palaces, public offices, hospitals, and private mansions. Catherine carefully examined the designs of court architects. She personally supervised the construction of the Marble Palace designed by the Italian Antonio Rinaldi for her favorite Grigory Orlov, and the Taurida Palace built by Ivan Starov for the distinguished statesman Prince Potemkin of Taurida. Dating from the same period is the Academy of Arts built by Alexander Kokorinov and Jean Baptiste Vallin de la Mothe in a style transitional between Baroque and Classicism. Toward the end of Catherine's reign the city's architecture became more reserved. The Academy of Sciences and the Issue Bank erected in the 1780s–1800s by the Italian Giacomo Quarenghi have the ascetic look typical of austere Classicism. Quarenghi became the favorite architect of Catherine II and was highly esteemed by her for his adherence to strict classical forms.

No effort was spared to build granite embankments, landing stages, descents to the water, and railings that turned the waterways into veritable artistic complexes. Chain bridges across the Fontanka and the "humpbacked" Swan Canal, Laundry and Hermitage Bridges were integrated into the single harmonious whole of the city center. Work on the Neva embankments was completed between 1770 and 1784 with the installation of a magnificent wrought-iron railing at the waterfront of the Summer Gardens, made to the design and under the supervision of Yuri Velten and Pyotr Egorov.

St. Michael's Castle, built by the Italian Vincenzo Brenna for Emperor Paul I between 1797 and 1800, was the last royal residence to appear in the eighteenth century. Haunted by fears and anxieties, Paul I conceived his palace as a medieval castle with moats full of water, drawbridges, and an enclosed inner courtyard. He also had an equestrian statue of Peter I placed in front of the main entrance. This romantic castle was fated to become the last abode of the Emperor who hastened its construction as if he knew what the future had in store for him. His presentiment came true: he was assassinated in the castle within months of its completion.

The first half of the nineteenth century was the heyday of Russian Classicism and also its final stage called the Empire style. The reigns of the two emperors, Alexander I and Nicholas I, which occupied the whole of this period, was marked by major achievements in urban development. The city grew rapidly. In the 1820s, it occupied an area of 76 sq km and had a population of 425,000.

The reign of Alexander I produced a number of outstanding architects of the Classical style, including Andrei Voronikhin, Adrian Zakharov, Thomas de Thomon, Carlo Rossi, and Vasily Stasov. They continued to work under Nicholas I and created magnificent architectural complexes in the downtown districts of St. Petersburg.

Among the finest examples of the Empire style are the Kazan Cathedral built by Voronikhin in 1801–11 on Nevsky Prospekt, the Admiralty reconstructed by Zakharov in 1806–23 and the Stock Exchange erected by Thomas de Thomon in 1804–10. These and other buildings in the "Alexander" classical style were to remain the architectural highlights of imperial St. Petersburg. The personality of Alexander I, a man of refined taste, contributed greatly to this flourishing of architecture and influenced the formation of the period style. He personally examined and approved the designs for all buildings, including private houses. Of great significance for the creation of the formal image of St. Petersburg was the completion of the capital's four central squares – Admiralty, Palace, St. Isaac's, and Senate Squares – integrated in a single architectural ensemble.

While Admiralty Square took its final shape after the reconstruction of the Admiralty, Palace Square acquired its present-day form in 1819–29 after the reconstruction of the General Staff Headquarters and the Ministries of Finance and Foreign Affairs by Carlo Rossi and the installation in the center of the square of the Alexander Column designed by Auguste Montferrand. Between 1829 and 1834 Rossi erected two more buildings – the Senate and the Synod. Linked by an arch, they formed the west side of Senate Square, turning it into a pleasantly harmonious whole. In the mid-nineteenth century another square, St. Isaac's, was added to the already established network of three squares; it was completed in 1858 when the enormous St. Isaac's Cathedral, designed by Montferrand, reached its final 100-meter height here. St. Isaac's Square was one of the last classical complexes created in St. Petersburg including, besides the cathedral, Lobanov-Rostovsky's mansion (1817–19, architect Montferrand) and the Mariinsky Palace (1839–44, architect Stakenschneider). Between 1856 and 1859, a monument to Nicholas I was set up in the center of the square (architect Montferrand, sculptor Klodt).

Of great importance was the reconstruction of Nevsky Prospekt, the central street of the city. This work began in 1818 with Carlo Rossi's building for Nicholas I's brother Mikhail of the palace which now houses the Russian Museum.

Another architectural complex, created by Rossi in 1816–32 and also opening onto Nevsky Prospekt, included the Alexandrinsky Theater with Theater Square in front of it, Theater Street (made up like Uffizi Street in Florence of two identical rows of buildings) and a square near the Chernyshov Bridge (now Lomonosov Square). A whole system of streets and squares was thus created linking Nevsky Prospekt to other districts of the city.

Building of the ensembles in the city center was completed in the reign of Nicholas I, whose personal tastes also left their mark on the character of architecture, but unlike Alexander I, Nicholas I gave preference to stylized architecture in the spirit of Romanticism, and to what is known as the Russian style in particular. This style was represented mostly by religious structures designed by Konstantin Thon whose work echoed the well-known ideological concept: Orthodoxy, Autocracy and Nationality *(narodnost)*.

The reign of Nicholas I marked the end of aristocratic domination in Russian history. From the mid nineteenth century began the era of the bourgeois development of the country. This period was also a turning point in the history of St. Petersburg. The city rapidly grew into a major industrial center, with gigantic factories, such as the Putilov, Obukhov and Baltic Works, emerging on its outskirts. New industrial enterprises surrounded the city center in a semicircle, gradually cutting it off from the suburbs and the sea. The intensive development of industry led to a rise in population due to the inflow of people from other parts of the country. While in 1860 the city had a population of 500,000, at the beginning of the twentieth century it had increased to 1,5 million and at the outbreak of the First World War it had reached over 2 million, making St. Petersburg the ninth largest city in the world.

The growth of population accelerated the rate of housing construction. Large apartment houses appeared in many districts, leaving a stamp on their architectural appearance. The former aristocratic center was gradually turning into the business, commercial and financial center of a big capitalist city. Banks, railway stations, trading houses, churches and public offices were built everywhere.

New bridges spanned rivers and canals, the most important of which were the permanent drawbridges across the Neva such as the Liteiny Bridge (architect Krakau, engineer Struve), Troitsky, Palace and Okhta Bridges.

In the early twentieth century, buildings in the Art Nouveau style began to appear in St. Petersburg and some other European cities. While in the downtown districts, on Nevsky Prospekt and St. Isaac's Square, isolated structures of this kind did not change the essential character of the area, in other parts of the city, especially on the Petrograd Side, an important construction site of that time, Art Nouveau and neoclassical houses became a dominant element. The best architects of the Art Nouveau style include Alexander Gogen, Alfred Parland, Fedor Lidval, Gavriil Baranovsky, and Pyotr Suzor. Among their best creations are the House of the Singer Company and Eliseyev's grocery shop on Nevsky Prospekt, the Astoria Hotel, and some others.

In the 1910s, almost at the same time as the Art Nouveau style, a new movement emerged in architecture, known as neoclassicism or retrospectivism. Architects once again derived inspiration from the past, striving to preserve the artistic integrity of St. Petersburg. Their designs, recreating the forms of the eighteenth and early nineteenth centuries, were intended to further Peter I's westernizing tendencies, and their vision was of St. Petersburg as a renovated Europeanized city.

The buildings of the Russian Trade and Industry Bank on Nevsky Prospekt (1910–15, architect Marian Peretyatkovich), the Azov-Don Commercial Bank in Bolshaya Morskaya Street (1907–10, architect Fedor Lidval), the House of the Guards Economic Society (1908–09, architect Ernest Virrich), the Martens Trading House on Nevsky Prospekt (1910–13, architect Marian Lialevich) are the finest examples of the neoclassical style.

The reigns of the last three emperors of Russia, Alexander II, Alexander III and Nicholas II, covering the second half of the nineteenth and the beginning of the twentieth centuries, were a time of free capitalist growth and the emperors' personalities did not directly influence the architectural development of the city, except in some minor ways. Thus, Alexander III was notable for his love of the pseudo-Russian style both in architecture and everyday life.

In the early twentieth century the enterprising spirit of the time manifested itself not so much in architecture as in the general life style of the metropolis, turbulent and diverse. Flashy commercial advertisements, shop-signs, lights of numerous movie-houses almost entirely covered the facades of buildings, overshadowing their architecture. Yet, despite the diversity of architectural styles, St. Petersburg has always been an integral city with different historical periods organically blending to create a harmonious whole, its dominant feature being the classical "stately aspect and perfect ranks." The panorama of St. Petersburg, as recorded by the artist Bernardazzi more than a hundred years ago, confirms this opinion and clearly shows that the city, standing on the threshold of its tercentenary, remains as modern as ever.

*Pages from History*
*1    7    0    3    ◆    1    9    1    7*

# Peter I, The Great

## Last Tsar of Muscovy and First Emperor of All The Russias
## Founder of St. Petersburg, The New Russian Capital

REIGNED

1 6 8 2 · 1 7 2 5

The city born on the banks of the Neva River "to the crash of axes and the thunder of cannon" paradoxically combined within itself over the course of centuries the cold majesty of an imperial capital and the hot spirit of rebellion inherited from the man by whose will it was created – Emperor Peter the Great, who himself became a symbol of a new Russia. ■ Even in his outward appearance Peter bore little resemblance to the majority of contemporary rulers. He was over six foot three inches tall and possessed immense physical strength. He had a marked fondness for hard work and a simple life style. He was a skillful carpenter, talented shipbuilder and naval commander, and an accomplished diplomat. During his reign Russia opened its first permanent missions abroad. ■ Yet at the same time Peter was quick-tempered and cruel, with no qualms about ordering executions. ■ His reforms were received with implacable hostility by a sizable number of people. Among those who fell victim to his determination to overcome this opposition was his own son Alexei. ■ The changes Peter introduced affected all aspects of life in the country. The very apparatus of state was reformed: the Boyar Duma (the council of boyars) was replaced by the Senate created in 1711; numerous *prikazy* (departments, offices) gave way to collegia, or colleges, the direct forerunners of later ministries; in 1721, the office of patriarch was discontinued with the foundation of the *Dukhovnaya Collegia*, or the Holy Synod, under government control. ■ With the aim of strengthening the merchant class Peter founded the *Burmisterskaya Palata* (an organ of municipal administration) and municipal magistrates. Manufacturing and mining enterprises appeared in the country and the exploitation of new iron-ore deposits was begun. The promulgation of the Table of Ranks in 1722 made it possible for a man to advance himself in society not on account of noble origins, but through his abilities and services rendered. ■ In his desire to imitate the West and to do away with old Russian customs, the tsar forbade the wearing of the traditional long-skirted Russian costume, replacing it with styles of dress borrowed from Hungary, France, Saxony and other parts of Germany. Tailors and merchants who produced or sold Russian costumes were flogged and condemned to penal servitude. Those

PORTRAIT OF EMPEROR PETER I

*18th century*
*By an unknown artist*
*Oil on canvas*
*66 x 53*

*The portrait shows Peter I wearing a caftan with a ribbon of the Order of St. Andrew the First-Called.*

who continued to sport the traditional beard had to pay dearly for the privilege – Peter introduced a punitive beard tax in return for which a man would receive a special token as proof of his right not to shave. ■ In the nineteenth century the Russian historian Mikhail Pogodin wrote that Peter had introduced into Russian life "a place in the system of European states, administration, legal proceedings, the rights of the estates, the Table of Ranks, the army, the navy, taxes, the census, conscription, factories, works, harbors, canals, roads, post offices, agriculture, forestry, animal husbandry, mining, gardening, viniculture, internal and external trade, clothing, looks, pharmacies, hospitals, medicines, the calendar, language, printing, military colleges, academies…" ■ But neither contemporaries nor subsequent generations were unanimous in their assessment of this man's contribution to Russian life. Even today the arguments about the damage and benefit of Peter's transformations to the country and its people still continue. One thing, however, is certain: his creation of the city on the Neva initiated the tremendously significant "St. Petersburg period in Russian history." ■ The appearance of St. Petersburg was a consequence of the Northern War which Russia waged for 21 years in order to recover the former Russian lands along the Neva and the Gulf of Finland which Sweden had seized in the early seventeenth century. ■ In 1699, Peter began forming the first regiments of a regular Russian army. Earlier still, in 1696, the creation of a fleet on the Sea of Azov had laid the foundations for Russia's navy. ■ On 22 August 1700, the Muscovite state embarked on the war from which it was to emerge in 1721 as the victorious and powerful Russian Empire. ■ For Russia the war began with a defeat near Narva. It was a harsh lesson which led Peter to declare a new round of conscription into the army. Factories were constructed in the Urals to produce urgently needed weapons. The shipyards began to create the Russian navy which by the end of Peter's reign was one of the most powerful in the world. Everything in the country was subordinated to the needs of the army. ■ And from January 1702 onwards, the Russian forces went from victory to victory. The Tsar personally participated in many of the battles. For his part in the first maritime victory on 7 May 1702 Peter himself was awarded the highest Russian decoration, the newly-instituted Order of the Holy Apostle Andrew the First-Called. ■ The foundation on 16 (27) May 1703 of the St. Petersburg Fortress on Zayachy (Hare) Island in the delta of the Neva marked the consolidation of Russian power on the shores of the Baltic for once and for all. That day saw the beginning of a city which, like the fortress, was named in honor of the Tsar's patron saint – Peter, the keeper of the keys to Paradise – a city which was intended to become the key to the Promised Land on the Baltic. Later, when a cathedral dedicated to the Holy Apostles Peter and Paul was constructed in the fortress, it came to be known by both their names (officially only since 1858), while the city which grew up around it retained the older name, St. Petersburg. ■ The site for the new fortress was carefully selected. The size and shape of Zayachy Island – about 750 meters long and 360 wide – made it possible to use the whole of it for the fortress, thus depriving the enemy of the chance of coming ashore on the island itself. The Neva, while being the shortest of all the major European rivers (74 kilometers long), is one of the greatest in terms of volume of water with a depth of 8–11 meters and an average current of 1.2 meters a second, and formed a formidable natural defence for the fortress. ■ The new city grew rapidly. The whole of Russia worked on it to the cracking of whips. Noblemen, merchants and craftsmen were forcibly resettled here. Each new inhabitant was obliged by Peter's command to build himself a house in accordance with his rank and wealth. The first material used was wood, but in 1714 construction of stone buildings began in St. Petersburg, while it was forbidden in the rest of the country. One of the first inhabitants of the city was the Tsar himself. In the space of three days carpenter soldiers assembled a small log cabin for him on the bank of the Neva and on 28 May 1703 Peter was able to move in. ■ The majority of the city's population was made up of those who had been forced to come here – stonemasons, carpenters, joiners, metalworkers, tailors, coopers, tradesmen etc. Quite a large number of foreigners made the city their permanent home – Germans, Dutchmen, Englishmen, and Danes. These were naval officers, craftsmen, doctors, pharmacists, and teachers, many of whom lived the rest of their lives in Russia. ■ They usually took up residence in areas according to their trade or national origin. Some of the places and street names in St. Petersburg today still remind us of the people who once lived there. ■ By 1725 the city already had more than 40,000 inhabitants. ■ As St. Petersburg was built up and its population grew, the city's infrastructure developed and became more complex, obliging Peter to address himself seriously to questions of municipal administration. A decree of 1718 created a head of the city police with a department under him. The police had responsibility for supervising construction of the city, the cleanliness of the streets, the consolidation of river and canal banks, order in public places and trade in foodstuffs. Fire precautions and fire-fighting were a particular concern of the police since fires were a real calamity. ■ In selecting a site for Russia's new capital Peter was guided by goals of military strategy and politics and paid no heed to the unfavorable natural environment of the locality – low-lying marshland either side of the Neva, subject to annual flooding. In the very year when the city was founded, in August 1703, the waters of the Neva rose by more than two meters. In the 290 years since the river has risen more than 300 times. The most serious floods occurred in 1777 when the water climbed 3.10 meters above the many-year average level for the lower reaches of the river; 1824 – 4.10 meters; and 1924 – 3.69 meters. ■ In 1704, only a year after the foundation of the fortress-city, in a letter written to St. Petersburg's first governor, Prince Alexander Menshikov, Peter called the city the capital. But the final acknowledgement of St. Petersburg as the capital of Russia came only in 1712. That year saw the festive celebration in St. Petersburg of Peter's marriage to Martha Skavronskaya, the future Empress Catherine I. The royal court moved here as did many foreign ambassadors. In 1713, the Senate and many other state institutions moved to St. Petersburg and from that moment on the city became not only the economic, but also the political center of the country. Peter also strove to make it a national center of learning and culture. The new Russia had need of qualified people for industry, the army and the navy. New educational establishments appeared in St. Petersburg: the Naval Academy, Schools of Engineering and Artillery. These were open to the sons of a range of classes. For noblemen's children, though, education and subsequent service to the state were compulsory. A decree of 1714 established that any nobleman who did not attain the basic level of knowledge required for state service was forbidden to marry. This provision was confirmed by the 1722 decree "On the Attestation of Fools in the Senate." ■ St. Petersburg became a center for book printing. The first Russian printed newspaper, *Vedemosti (News)*, appeared in Moscow in 1703 and from 1711 onward it was published in St. Petersburg. The first public library in the country appeared in St.

Petersburg, while Peter's private library in the Summer Palace later became the foundation for the library of the Academy of Sciences which was established at Peter's command in 1724. The Tsar had long cherished the idea of creating a center of learning for the country. He himself was unanimously elected a member of the Parisian Academy of Sciences in 1717 and strove to have an academy of his own in St. Petersburg. The Russian body differed from its foreign counterparts in the range of disciplines it embraced and its secular character. The Academy enjoyed a high reputation in Europe and world-renowned scholars, such as Leonhard Euler and Daniel Bernoulli, were to work there. ■ Peter was a patron of the fine arts and of the theater, including folk theater. The Emperor's sister, Natalia Alexeyevna, organized a theater in St. Petersburg and herself wrote plays of a secular character for it. ■ Over the years the way of life of the Russian noble and merchant classes changed. Outwardly the aristocrats could no longer be distinguished from those of Western Europe. The position of women in society was transformed. All the wives and daughters of the nobility were obliged to lead a social life, to organize receptions, to go out for drives and to attend the assemblies which were instituted by the Tsar's special decree in 1718. ■ As Russia's position in the Northern War grew stronger, the importance of the northern capital also grew. In 1719, military operations moved to Swedish territory. The Peace of Nystadt concluded on 30 August 1721 confirmed Russia, by then a world-ranking naval power, in uncontested possession of the lands along the Baltic. On 22 October 1721, at a celebratory session of the Senate, the chancellor Gavriil Golovkin asked the Tsar to accept the title of "Father of the Nation, Peter the Great, Emperor of All the Russias." In this way Russia officially became an empire, and its ruler the emperor of a mighty realm.

"Mirror."

*2nd half of the 18th century Cast ormolu. 29 x 29 x 50*

*Introduced by Peter I, this table showcase bearing the State Emblem of Russia on its sides was used to display the Emperor's three major decrees:*

*1. On Protection of Civil Rights (April 17, 1722)*
*2. On Behavior in Court (January 21, 1724)*
*3. On State Regulations and Their Importance (January 22, 1724)*
*Every administrative office in Russia was supposed to have a*

*similar showcase in the 18th and 19th centuries.*
*The crowns above the heads of the double-headed eagles were removed in the 1930s following the ideological campaign against symbols of autocracy.*

Домикъ Петра Великаго.    Maisonnette de Pierre le Grand.

### PETER I'S LOG CABIN

*1816*
*Engraving by Stepan Galaktionov from a drawing by Pyotr Svinin*
*19 x 24*

On May 28, 1703, the first housewarming was celebrated in St. Petersburg. In the space of three days soldier carpenters built Peter I the first house of the future capital out of logs. Inside the walls were hung with canvas, outside they were painted in imitation of brick. The cabin is small, with a study, dining room, bedroom, and entrance-hall. Following Peter's death, the building was protected from the elements by a roofed gallery and under Catherine II the cabin was enclosed by a stone pavilion.

### PETER I ON LAKE LADOGA DURING A STORM

*First half of the 19th century*
*By an unknown artist from the original of 1820 by Carl Steuben*
*Oil on canvas*
*102 x 123*

This work depicts one of the dramatic episodes in the life of Peter I. The St. Petersburg seaport received cargo from the interior regions of Russia by a water system which included a dangerous section on Lake Ladoga. River vessels were not adapted for lake navigation and Peter ordered a by-pass canal to be built along the southern shore of the lake. In 1724, Peter I set out in a small sailboat to survey the work on the canal excavation when he was unexpectedly caught in a storm. Wind broke the mast, waves flooded the boat, and the oarsmen panicked. Only the courage and self-possession of the Tsar, taking the rudder in his hands, saved the vessel.

THE MARRIAGE OF PETER I AND CATHERINE I ON

*February 19, 1712*
*1712*
*Engraving by Alexei Zubov*
*52 x 71*

*The marriage of Peter I and Catherine I took place in the large hall
of the first Winter Palace in St. Petersburg. In the foreground (no. 2),
Catherine sits in a company of ladies. Further back (no. 1), Peter I is
in the center amongst the men. Alexei Zubov, one of the best engravers
of Peter's time, minutely recorded the interior: tapestries, mirrors,
lamps, and the details of the wedding table.*

ВИДЪ НЕВСКАГО МОНАСТЫРЯ. с.п.б.г 1815 г. VUE DE COUVENT DE NEVSKY A St PETERSBOURG.

THE ALEXANDER NEVSKY LAVRA FROM THE NEVA

*1815*
*Engraving tinted with watercolor by Ivan Ivanov*
*51 x 65.5*

This monastery was founded by order of Peter I in 1710 on the site where, according to legend, Prince Alexander Nevsky defeated the Swedish army in 1241. Its general plan was worked out by Domenico Trezzini, one of the first architects of St. Petersburg. In 1724, the relics of the saintly, pious Prince Alexander Nevsky were transferred to the monastery and Peter I took part in this solemn ceremony. Under him, the Alexander Nevsky Monastery occupied a position higher than that of all other Orthodox monasteries in Russia. A printing press, school, seminary and, later, an ecclesiastical academy were opened here. The Church of the Annunciation was a burial place for members of the royal family and distinguished Petersburg residents. Seen beyond the railing is the cupola of the Trinity Cathedral erected to a design by Ivan Starov between 1776 and 1790. The monastery received the status of lavra (the highest Orthodox rank) in 1797.

INTERIOR OF THE KUNSTKAMMER (CABINET OF CURIOS)

*1741*
*Engraving by Grigory Kachalov*
*57.5 x 72.5*

While traveling in Europe, Peter I acquired every possible kind of rarity as well as books and art objects. In 1714, on the basis of his collections the first museum in Russia was created. After Peter's death, this museum was transferred to the Kunstkammer, built between 1718 and 1734 on Vasilyevsky Island.

ICON OF THE SAINTLY MOST ORTHODOX GRAND PRINCE
ALEXANDER NEVSKY WHO, IN 1240, LAUNCHED A CAMPAIGN
AGAINST THE TEUTONIC KNIGHT CRUSADERS IN DEFENCE
OF THE ORTHODOX FAITH IN RUSSIAN LANDS

*2nd half, 19th century. Germany*
*Porcelain, overglaze painting*
*28 x 22*

*The icon was previously in the Peter and Paul Cathedral. To
emphasize the importance of the new capital, Peter I founded the
Alexander Nevsky Monastery and in 1724 ordered that the
imperishable relics of Alexander Nevsky, who was canonized in
1380, be transferred to St. Petersburg. In 1725, the relics were
brought to the monastery. Empress Elizabeth I donated a silver
shrine for the relics, which is now displayed in the Hermitage
(without the relics). In 1725, a new decoration was created in Russia
to honor this saint.*

VIEW OF THE FIREWORKS IN AMSTERDAM ON DECEMBER 9, 1721 MARKING THE CONCLUSION OF THE TREATY OF NYSTADT

*1720s*
*Engraving by John Smith*
*53.2 x 61*

*On August 30, 1721 in Nystadt, Finland, a peace was concluded between Russia and Sweden. By its provisions the land captured from Sweden was permanently ceded to Russia. Celebrations marking the Treaty were held in St. Petersburg and Moscow. Fireworks commemorating the peace settlement were also organized by Russian ambassadors in a number of Western European countries. One such display, represented in this engraving, took place in Amsterdam.*

THE CEREMONIAL ENTRY INTO ST. PETERSBURG IN 1714 OF THE CAPTURED SWEDISH SQUADRON

*1714*
*Engraving by Peter Pickaerdt*
*71 x 93*

*Depicted is the celebration of the Russian fleet's victory over the Swedes off Grönhamn, the Åland Islands harbor. Captive Swedish ships float on the Neva and captive soldiers are being led onto Trinity Square which received its name from the church founded in 1704 and was the city's central square at the beginning of the 18th century.*
*The highest organs of government – the Governing Senate and the Collegia (ministries) – were located here and goods were stored in the building of Gostiny Dvor.*

### THE CORONATION OF CATHERINE I

*Late 19th century*
*Heliogravure from an engraving of 1724 by Ivan Zubov*
*75 x 87.5*

An allegorical picture presented to Catherine I by academics on the occasion of her coronation in 1724. In the upper part, Peter I is depicted wearing a laurel wreath, and behind him are the figures of Neptune, Hercules and Glory. On the right, accompanied by six goddesses, is Catherine I and a cartouche with a dedication to the Empress.

### EPIPHANY FESTIVAL ON ON JANUARY 6 (19, NEW STYLE), 1727

*Second quarter of the 19th century. Tinted lithograph*
*23.5 x 34.5*

On the Neva ice, next to an ice-hole, a rotunda called a "Jordan," was built, where the rite of the consecration of water was enacted. This lithograph shows the ceremonial procession of horse-guardsmen accompanying the carriage of Empress Catherine I on the Neva ice.

*Кавалергардія въ церемоніалъ шествія Императрицы Екатерины I, въ день Крещенскаго парада, 6 Января 1727.*

# Anna I Ioannovna

REIGNED

1 7 3 0  1 7 4 0

The death of Peter the Great began the "age of palace coups" in Russia, when over a period of 37 years the imperial throne was occupied by a rapid succession of sovereigns. On several occasions it was not only the crown and the continuance of Peter's reforms which were at stake but also the destiny of St. Petersburg as the capital of the empire. ■ A decisive role in these palace coups was played by the guards, the elite units of the regular army which Peter had personally created. It was their support which enabled Anna Ioannovna, Peter's niece and the widowed Duchess of Courland (western Latvia), to become Russia's autocratic ruler in 1730. In 1732, Anna brought the royal court back to St. Petersburg. By that time Peter's beloved brainchild had been completely abandoned. When Peter II, Anna's predecessor, moved to Moscow in 1728 St. Petersburg effectively ceased to be the capital. The population began to drift away, construction came to a halt, the factories closed and trade and industry were deprived of state support. But when the imperial court returned to St. Petersburg the population started to grow once again. In the 1730s, it numbered more than 68,000 people. ■ The construction of the city was resumed. Large sums of money were directed toward the completion of edifices begun in Peter's time such as the build-

PORTRAIT OF EMPRESS ANNA
IOANNOVNA

*1730*
*Engraving tinted with watercolor by*
*Christian Albrecht Wortmann from a*
*portrait by Louis Caravaque*
*35 x 24*

*The Empress is shown wearing a small*
*crown with the chain of the Order of*
*St. Andrew the First-Called. Below are*
*the state coat of arms and the large*
*imperial crown.*

ing of the Twelve Colleges, the *Kunstkammer* (Cabinet of Curios) and the reconstruction in stone of the Peter and Paul Fortress. ■ After the major fires of 1736 and 1737 which caused much damage in the city, a Commission for the Construction of St. Petersburg was set up. The commission decided to divide the city into administrative areas to be headed by police offices responsible for amenities and order in their districts. ■ Empress Anna's reign began under the slogan of a return to the policy of Peter I. A wax figure of the great reformer created by the Italian sculptor Carlo Rastrelli was festively installed in the *Kunstkammer* – the first Russian museum. But gradually in domestic affairs the collective decision-making of Peter's time gave way to individual rule. In 1731, a three-man Cabinet of Ministers was instituted with Andrei Ostermann at its head and placed above the Senate. Power in the country passed into the hands of the Baltic Germans who had arrived with

Anna Ioannovna from Courland. They enjoyed the Empress's unlimited trust and were appointed to key posts of state: Burkhard Christoph Munnich became president of the Army College, A. Schemberg chief administrator of the mining industry, Baron Mengden head of the College of Commerce, and so on. They were followed to Russia by their relatives who installed themselves in profitable posts. Immense power was wielded by the Empress's lover Ernst-Johann Biron. ■ The Empress was extremely fond of festivities and spent enormous sums on balls, masquerades, fireworks displays, and other amusements. Even foreigners were staggered by the opulence of her court. The Duke de Liria, Spanish ambassador to the Russian court, left us a description of the Empress: "She is fat, rather swarthy, and her face is more masculine than feminine… She is generous to the point of extravagance and loves luxury to excess, for which reason the splendor of her court exceeds all others in Europe." ■ The Empress had a particular weakness for certain types of living curiosities. She maintained at court a huge number of dwarves, giants, rare animals, and birds. She also had a host of male and female jesters in her retinue and comic parades were another favorite amusement. The most remarkable of these was in 1740 on the occasion of the marriage between a court jester called Kvasnik and a female colleague, a Kalmyk woman called Buzheninova, which took place in an Ice House built on the frozen surface of the Neva between the Winter Palace and the Admiralty. The memoirs of one contemporary include a detailed description of this wonderful edifice and its contents: tables, chairs, beds, tableware, clocks, and other objects – all made of ice and colored with "natural dyes." Cannon made of ice were set up in front of the Ice House and salvoes fired from them. Ice dolphins stood by the gate spouting fiery fountains of burning oil. An ice elephant squirted a jet of water from its trunk by day and a jet of fire by night. In the same area there was an ice bathhouse, in which visitors to the Ice House took steam baths. The newlyweds were congratulated by representatives of all the peoples living in Russia who had been specially brought to the capital for this purpose. The wedding procession was a living ethnographic exhibition. ■ In the meantime, while the Empress devoted herself to amusements, dissatisfaction was growing among the Russian nobility and the common people. The nobles were disturbed by the spread of foreign, chiefly German, influence at court, while the people had to bear the intolerable burden of new taxes to replenish the state's constantly empty coffers. The firm position which Peter the Great had won for Russia in the international arena was lost during Anna's reign, and that provoked discontent among the officers and the guards. ■ On 17 October 1740 the Empress died, having bequeathed the throne to the two-month-old son of her niece Anna Leopoldovna. Biron was appointed to be regent with unlimited powers over the foreign and domestic affairs of Russia until the infant emperor attained his seventeenth birthday. ■ But the public mood left the favorite with a very fragile grip on power and the series of palace coups which followed. Empress Anna's death eventually brought Peter the Great's daughter Elizabeth to the throne.

THE TWELVE COLLEGIA BUILDING ON VASILYEVSKY
ISLAND

*Mid 18th century*
*Engraving tinted with watercolor by R. Wilkinson from a drawing*
*by Mikhail Makhayev*
*34.5 x 49*

*Depicted are two civil buildings of Peter's epoch erected by Domenico*
*Trezzini in the 1730s on the Spit of Vasilyevsky Island: on the left is*
*the building of the Twelve Collegia which housed Russia's supreme*
*government ministries. (In 1819, the entire complex was transferred*
*to St. Petersburg University, which is still located here today.) On the*
*right is Gostiny Dvor, a storehouse for imported and exported goods.*
*The St. Petersburg seaport was situated nearby. Decrees were*
*proclaimed and executions took place on this square.*

ILLUMINATION IN FRONT OF THE ACADEMY OF SCIENCES
TO MARK ITS GRAND ASSEMBLY

*1749*
*Engraving by Ivan Sokolov from a sketch by Elias Grimmel*
*24.2 x 35.5*

*The St. Petersburg Academy of Sciences was founded by Peter I in
1724.*

TEAPOT, TRAY AND CANDLESTICK. 1ST QUARTER, 18TH
CENTURY

*Enamel, plated silver*
*Height of teapot 10, tray 20 x 16, height of candlestick 14*

*Rare examples of 18th-century household utensils, made of metal and
enamel at Veliky Ustiug, the center of this handicraft*

FIREWORKS IN FRONT OF THE WINTER PALACE ON
JANUARY 1, 1761

*1761. Engraving*
*49.5 x 63*

*Peter I introduced the custom of celebrating victories, various
achievements and of greeting the New Year with colorful, fiery
spectacles. Scholars at the Academy of Sciences provided the
composition and description of the display, while the technical work
and lighting of the fireworks was carried out by the Artillery
Department. Mythological and biblical scenes were used in allegorical
presentations.*

THE ADMIRALTY FROM NEVSKY PROSPEKT

*Third quarter of the 18th century*
*Painted copy by an unknown artist from an engraving of 1753*
*Oil on canvas*
*58 x 111*

---

*The Admiralty shipyard for the Baltic fleet was laid in 1704 to plans
by Peter I. In 1721, the mud-walled blocks of the Admiralty began to
be rebuilt in stone and between 1732 and 1738 the architect Ivan
Korobov reconstructed the central block and erected a new tower with
a golden spire and a ship-weathervane on top. From the central
tower of the Admiralty three major city thoroughfares radiate out:
Nevsky Prospekt, Gorokhovaya Street and Voznesensky Prospekt.
Nevsky Prospekt is the main street of the city, built in the 1710s as a
road connecting the Admiralty with the Novgorod highway
(approximately present-day Ligovsky Prospekt) and the Alexander
Nevsky Lavra.*

# Elizabeth

## (ELIZAVETA PETROVNA)

REIGNED

## 1741 — 1761

Another in the series of palace coups took place on 25 November 1741, bringing Peter the Great's daughter Elizabeth to the throne. Her accession caused a real explosion of national sentiment in Russian society. Again the guards played a decisive role in the coup and were generously rewarded with lands, serfs, titles, and ranks. The coronation took place on 25 April 1742 in the traditional place, the Dormition Cathedral of the Moscow Kremlin. ■ Many people have left us their opinions of Empress Elizabeth. All her contemporaries without exception were enraptured by her looks. "Elizabeth is a beauty, the like of whom I have rarely seen. She has amazing facial coloring, splendid eyes, a superb neck, and an incomparable figure," the Duke de Liria, the Spanish ambassador, wrote about the 18-year-old princess. Even the future Catherine II, when she first saw Elizabeth, by then 34, exclaimed: "Truly it was impossible then, that first time, not to be struck by her beauty and majestic bearing." Contemporaries also noted her passion for changes of clothing. All acknowledged the exceptional elegance of her costumes and her excellent taste. At her death Elizabeth left a wardrobe of 15,000 dresses, two chests of silk stockings and several thousand pairs of shoes. ■ But the Empress's morals were in sharp contrast to her divine appearance.

PORTRAIT OF EMPRESS ELIZAVETA PETROVNA

*Second half of the 18th century. By an unknown artist from the original of 1750 by Louis Caravaque*
*Oil on canvas*
*88 x 71*

*The Empress wears a small crown, ermine cloak and brocade dress with a brooch on the breast. On the blue ribbon is the Order of St. Andrew the First-Called.*

For all her love of opulence, she was misery and distinguished herself in hypocrisy and even cruelty. Unable to bear other women's triumphs, Elizabeth's did her best to humiliate rivals. Memoir-writers recalled, for example, that once when she had unsuccessfully dyed her hair, Elizabeth gave orders for all society ladies to have their heads shaved.

The question of power always remained the central one for the Empress. When she came to the throne, she suspended the death penalty in Russia, as if drawing a line between Anna's reign and her own. But her fear of losing power, of falling victim to yet another coup, forced the Secret Chancellery to uncover plot after plot and cruelly punish the "conspirators." In the minds of contemporaries these same fears explained the Empress's unusual daily routine – she was active at night and slept during the day, frequently changing her place of residence. ■ Demonstrating her right to the Russian throne as the Peter's heir, Elizabeth tried to return to the style of legislation and state institutions of her father's time. Most of the time, however, this had the appearance of blind imitation. ■ The Empress's close retinue should be given their due. The majority of the people around her who controlled Russia's destiny were, as a rule, talented and intelligent. For example, the successes Russia enjoyed in domestic affairs, the development of science and culture are connected with the names of Counts Pyotr and Ivan Shuvalov. The latter not only supported the great scholar Mikhail Lomonosov's idea of creating a university in Moscow, but was himself instrumental in making it a reality. He was also a founder of the Academy of Arts which he then headed for six years. Chancellor Alexei Bestuzhev-Riumin did much to strengthen the state's foreign policy.

Desiring to follow her father's example in all things, Elizabeth also concerned herself for the prestige of the northern capital. By the middle of her reign the population numbered about 95,000 people. The city was also growing in area. Elizabeth continued Empress Anna's policy of moving industrial buildings outside St. Petersburg. All the cemeteries within the city limits were closed and taverns were removed from the main streets. ■ In Elizabeth's reign the center of the city acquired the increasingly grand appearance which is reflected in Mikhail Makhayev's famous engravings published as a special album in 1753. At this time St. Petersburg recovered its significance as the industrial and trading center of the country. In 1744, the Imperial Porcelain Factory, later to become world-famous, was founded here. ■ Elizabeth had a particular passion for the theater, which had disappeared from the life of the capital after Peter's death. Empress Anna had tried to reintroduce theatrical spectacles at court, setting aside a special hall in the Winter Palace for the purpose. German, French and Italian companies were invited to come and perform. In 1750, Elizabeth issued a decree permitting the performance of Russian comedies in private houses. Another decree the following year established the Russian Theater, which was run by the first Russian playwright Alexander Sumarokov and Fedor Volkov, the founder of the first permanent Russian theater in Yaroslavl. Accordingly, it is 1751 which the famous Alexandrinsky Drama Theater in St. Petersburg regards as the beginning of its history. ■ For all that she looked on herself as the continuer of Peter's causes, Elizabeth in fact did little to further his memory.

ЗИМНІЙ ДВОРЕЦЪ СО СТОРОНЫ АДМИРАЛТЕЙСТВА.
PALAIS D'HIVER DU COTÉ DE L'AMIRAUTÉ.

THE WINTER PALACE VIEWED FROM THE ADMIRALTY

*Second half, 19th century*
*Lithograph by Schütz from a drawing by K. Sabath and S. Chifflart*
*38 x 46*

Петергофской Ея Императорскаго Величества дворецъ на берегу финландскаго Залива

въ тритцати верстахъ отъ Санктпетербурга.

Peterhoff. Maison de Plaisance de Sa Maj.té Imp.le de toutes les Russies &c. &c. &c.
Située sur le Golfe de Finlande à trente Verstes de S.t Peterbourg.

VIEW OF THE GREAT PALACE AT PETERHOF

*1761*
*Engraving by Nikita Chelnakov and Prokofy Artemyev from a*
*drawing by Mikhail Makhayev*
*48.5 x 134*

---

*Construction of Peterhof on the shore of the Gulf of Finland as a*
*monument to Russia's victories in the war with Sweden began after*
*1714. The natural conditions were conducive to the creation of a*
*splendid complex with the palace standing on the highest point in the*
*middle of the park. The palace is connected with the sea by a intricate*
*system of terraces, fountains and canals. The basic scheme for the*
*overall composition was conceived by Peter I. Under him, the palace*
*was a modest two-story building which in the following years was*
*considerably expanded. The engraving shows the palace after its*
*reconstruction by Bartolomeo Francesco Rastrelli in 1745–55.*

PANORAMA OF THE NEVA DOWNSTREAM FROM THE
WINTER PALACE AND THE ACADEMY OF SCIENCES

*1753*
*Engraving by Grigory Kachalov from a drawing by Mikhail*
*Makhayev*
*54 x 144.5*

To mark the 50th anniversary of the city, a series of prints from
drawings by Mikhail Makhayev was published. These prints provide
the opportunity to see buildings and vistas which have disappeared
forever, and to gain a sense of Petersburg life during the reign of
Empress Elizaveta Petrovna.
Carriages travel on the embankments and streets, trade is conducted,
goods are unloaded from an arriving ship, and boats and launches
scurry on the river. On the left is the Winter Palace, built earlier for
Empress Anna Ioannovna. Later, on its site, the new Winter Palace
was erected (now part of the Hermitage). Nearby is the Admiralty,
the largest shipyard in Russia at the time. On the right, on the shore of
Vasilyevsky Island, are two buildings which belonged to the Academy
of Sciences; the Kunstkammer (with the tower) was the first museum
in St. Petersburg.

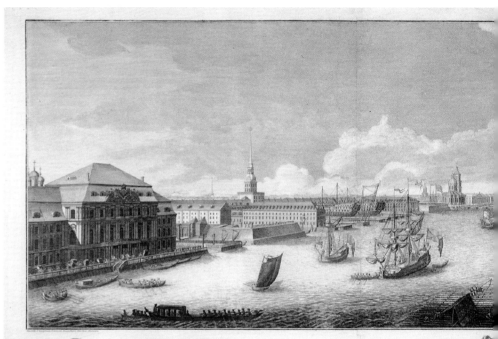

*Vue des bords de la Neva en descendant la rivière entre le Palais d'hiver de Sa Majesté Impériale & les batimens de l'Académie des Sciences*

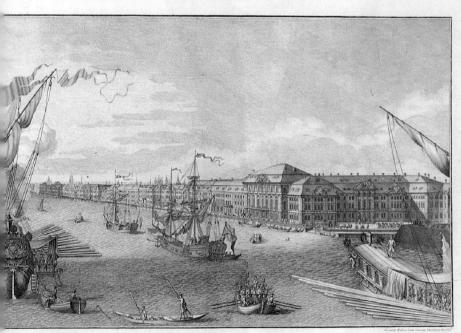

*Vue des bords de la Neva en remontant la rivière entre l'Amirauté et les batimens de l'Académie des Sciences.*

PANORAMA OF THE NEVA UPSTREAM FROM THE
ADMIRALTY AND THE ACADEMY OF SCIENCES

*1753*
*Engraving by Efim Vinogradov from a drawing by Mikhail Makhayev*
*56 x 141.5*

*In the center is a view of the Peter and Paul Fortress. Originally its walls were earthen, but even before the death of Peter I, the architect Domenico Trezzini began to rebuild it in stone. The fortress never took part in a single battle and with time its bastions were converted into a prison. The first prisoner was Tsarevich Alexei, accused for participating in a conspiracy against his father, Emperor Peter I. On the left is the old palace of Peter's sister-in-law, Praskovya Fedorovna, and on the right is a perspective of the Upper Embankment, which begins at the Winter Palace. Later, under Catherine II, the embankment was renamed Palace Embankment.*

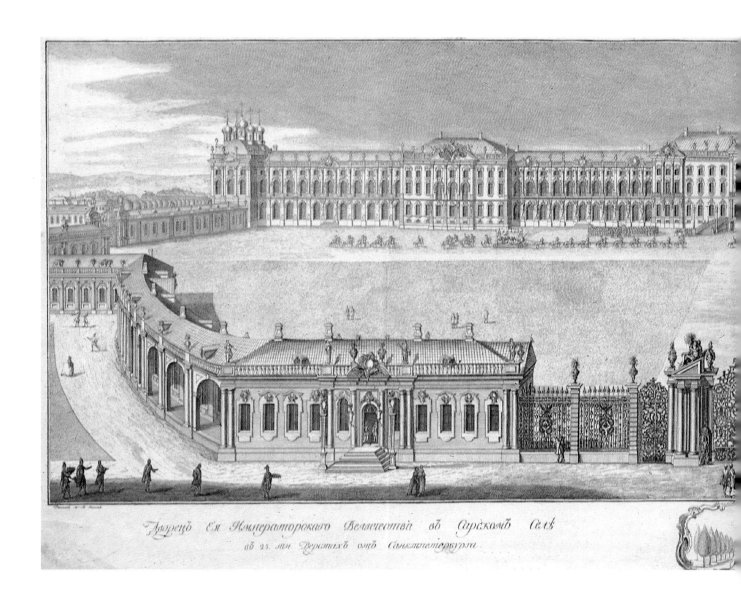

Дворецъ Ея Императорскаго Величества въ Арскомъ Селѣ
об 23 ми Верстахъ отъ Санктпетербурга.

VIEW OF THE GREAT PALACE AT TSARSKOYE SELO

*1761*
*Engraving by Nikita Chelnakov, Ekim Vnukov and Prokofy*
*Artemyev from a drawing by Mikhail Makhayev*
*50 x 134*
*In 1708, Peter I gave Tsarskoye Selo, in the environs of St.*
*Petersburg, as a gift to his wife Catherine, under whom a small two-*
*story stone palace was built here. In 1728, Tsarskoye Selo passed to*
*Peter's daughter Elizaveta Petrovna.*

*Having ascended the throne, Empress Elizaveta Petrovna chose*
*Tsarskoye Selo as her summer residence and built a huge palace*
*rivaling Versailles in its luxury. Construction was carried out by*
*Bartolomeo Francesco Rastrelli from 1752 to 1756. The palace*
*stunned contemporaries with its magnificent and ornate facades: all*
*the sculptural decoration from the caryatids to the vases and statues*
*on the roof's balustrade was gilded. This splendor did not end with*
*the exterior: endless suites of halls, gilded carvings reflected in*
*numerous mirrors, and the glimmer of thousands of candles all gave*
*the viewer the impression of a fantastic theatrical spectacle.*

Maison de Plaisance de sa Maj.te Imp.le de toutes les Russies &c. &c. &c.
à Sarskoe Selo, 25 Verstes de St. Petersbourg.

VIEW OF NEVSKY PROSPEKT TOWARD THE ADMIRALTY

*1753*
*Engraving tinted with watercolor by Yakov Vasilyev from a drawing*
*by Mikhail Makhayev*
*57.5 x 75.0*

*Left, across the bridge over the Fontanka River, is the Anichkov*
*Palace begun by Mikhail Zemtsov and Grigory Dmitriyev and*
*completed by Bartolomeo Francesco Rastrelli. A double gallery in*
*front of the palace and a canal from the Fontanka to an interior*
*pool have not survived. The palace was presented by Empress*
*Elizaveta Petrovna to her favorite, Count Alexei Razumovsky.*
*During the second half of the 19th century, the palace was one of the*
*permanent residences of Emperor Alexander III and his family.*

# Catherine II, The Great

REIGNED

## 1 7 6 2   1 7 9 6

The young princess from a small German principality whom Empress Elizabeth had selected as a bride for her nephew and chosen successor Peter traveled into the unknown of Russia in 1744 with a dream of a crown. "I wanted to be Russian so that the Russians would love me," she would write in her memoirs. Subsequently Empress Catherine II, having become a true Russian patriot, opened her own archives and those of the state to researchers: this resulted in the appearance of Vasily Tatishchev's famous *History of Russia from Earliest Times*. On 30 September 1783, encouraging the study and development of Russian language and literature, she signed a decree creating the Russian Academy to be headed by Princess Ekaterina Dashkova. ■ But first, when she arrived in Russia she made great efforts to learn Russian and the basic tenets of the Orthodox religion. As little as half a year later, when she received the name Ekaterina (Catherine) Alexeyevna at her Orthodox baptism, she impressed all present with her fine pronunciation of the Russian words of the service. ■ Catherine worked hard at her own education. She read Voltaire, Montesquieu and Bayle. Later she would recall that she read six books at the same time. Contemporaries were astonished by the Empress's fondness and capacity for work and drew comparisons with Peter the Great. ■ To a large extent this was a reflection of the character of a woman who had grown up with the conviction that she had to make her own way in life. The Russian historian Vasily Kliuchevsky observed: "She had a flexible and cautious mind… shrewdness, a feeling for the situation, strong powers of observation combined with an easy disposition. She was able to listen long and attentively, noting all the most positive aspects of people." ■ All these qualities helped Catherine to judge those around her, to assess their efficiency and competence. "I have no need of fools," the Empress declared categorically. ■ Real power always remained in the hands of Catherine herself. Even her numerous favorites, awarded ranks and decorations, were only permitted to decide secondary issues on their own initiative. In contrast to her female predecessors, Catherine II was never a pawn in someone else's game. Her ability to manoeuver and resist any form of pressure enabled her to

EMPRESS CATHERINE II

*Engraving by Joseph Lante from the original of 1762 by Stefano Torelli 62.5 x 33*

*The Empress is portrayed in coronation attire, wearing the large imperial crown and an ermine mantle with the chain of the Order of St. Andrew the First-Called over her left shoulder. Below, on the table, is a portrait of Grand Duke Pavel Petrovich with two sides of a coronation medal. The original was painted by Stefano Torelli to commemorate Catherine's coronation on September 22, 1762.*

avoid threats to her monopoly of power even from the participants in the coup of 28 June 1762 which brought her to the Russian throne. ■ The Empress saw her chief support as coming from the Russian nobility in all its different gradations. There are sound reasons why the reign of Catherine II has gone down in history as the golden age of the Russian nobility. ■ Soon after Catherine had taken the throne, the Governing Senate passed a decision to immortalize her in a monument. But the Empress proved cleverer than all her senators. She decided to erect a monument to Peter the Great and in doing so to declare herself the continuer of his causes. Peter was Catherine's political ideal… ■ In examining the foreign policy of the state under Catherine II it should be noted that, for all the debatable nature of its results, Russia did succeed in regaining the status of a great power which had been lost after Peter's death. As Prince Alexander Bezborodko, a leading diplomat of Catherine's time, observed: "… not a single cannon in Europe dared to fire without our permission." Much of this Russia owed to the great deeds of her soldiers and sailors led at that time by such remarkable commanders as Alexander Rumiantsev, Alexander Suvorov and Fedor Ushakov, men with many victories to their credit. ■ Like Peter the Great's transformations, Catherine II's reforms affected many aspects of the internal order in Russia and found reflection in the life of the capital, too. ■ In the course of Catherine's reign St. Petersburg turned into one of the most attractive cities in Europe. The tasks of the Committee for Masonry Construction, created by the Empress's decree in 1762, included compiling basic principles for the building of towns and cities and drawing up general plans for them. The committee devoted particular attention to the capital of the empire. Open competitions were announced for the creation of an overall scheme for the city and for Palace Square. This same period saw the embankments of the Neva faced in granite, the construction of the first stone bridges in the city and an improvement in street lighting. Pavements made of stone slabs were laid along the main streets of the city. In the 1790s, house numbers were introduced and pillars carrying street signs were set up. ■ By 1790 the population of St. Petersburg had grown to 220,000. At that time the male inhabitants were twice as numerous as the females due to the influx of workers from other parts of Russia. About a quarter of the entire population were members of the forces or their families. ■ Under Catherine St. Petersburg became the mighty industrial and trading center of the country. The already established development of military industry and shipbuilding continued. But at the same time business emerged to satisfy the needs of the broad mass market, such as weaving mills, tanneries and brickworks. A significant role was played by the manufacture of glass, porcelain and pottery as well as the cutting of precious and semiprecious stones. Small-scale manufacturing also expanded: by 1790 St. Petersburg had 56 Russian-owned and 36 foreign craft workshops producing an immense variety of items. ■ St. Petersburg was Russia's chief port handling more than half of all the country's foreign trade. Between 1775 and 1792 vessels from 18 different countries called at St. Petersburg. Arcades of shops, trading rows and stalls could be found in all parts of the city, as well as 14 markets. ■ The development of industry and trade demanded an expansion of finance, the creation of banks and exchanges. In this period the Exchange in the capital was the only one for the whole country. Banks issuing notes and loans began to appear. ■ New organs of government, the Offices for Public Care, were introduced in the reform of 1775 and given control of schools, hospitals, orphanages, almshouses, and reformatories. In 1784, the Office in St. Petersburg established the capital's first municipal hospital. Much attention was devoted to fighting epidemics. In order to encourage the use of vaccination, Catherine had herself and the heir to the throne inoculated against smallpox. ■ A reform in 1782 did away with the department of the police head in St. Petersburg and replaced it with the *Uprava Blagochiniya* (a police-like body charged with maintaining *blagochinie*, good order). From this moment on the city police were subordinated not to the Senate but to the Governor-General while retaining their former functions in the administration of the city's infrastructure. These consisted in observing the state of bridges and embankments, allocating land for further construction, and superintending sanitary conditions and the upkeep of the city. The *Uprava* had charge of the municipal fire-brigade which had been created in 1763. ■ A wider range of municipal government issues were covered in the 1785 *Zhalovannaya Gramota* (Charter to the Cities) of which Catherine herself was the chief author. This document established the rights and privileges of the cities for the first time. It consolidated the municipalities' property rights over land which they held and they received the right to have schools, mills, eating-places, inns and to organize fairs. All the inhabitants of cities, including the nobles, had certain fixed obligations and duties to pay and these could not be arbitrarily increased by the local authorities. The whole population of a city was divided into six categories, four of which covered those engaged in trade and industry, while the two others were mixed. The new organs of municipal self-administration were the city councils or *dumas*: the general duma and the "six-member" duma. The general duma was made up of deputies elected at gatherings of different groups, while the "six-member" duma was elected by representatives of the general duma and consisted of six men, one from each category of the population. The first elections for the duma took place in St. Petersburg on 21 January 1786. ■ Catherine's extensive reforming activities in the administration of the state were inseparably bound up with the development of learning and culture in the country. Her striving to reconcile the ideology of the Enlightenment with the conditions of a state based on serfdom, for all its contradictory nature, did indeed have some positive results. Everything which bore the stamp of the Enlightenment was an object of particular interest to Catherine. This included the publication of the works of the French *philosophes* and an enormous number of journals and the development of the Russian theater where the Empress herself was among the playwrights. Catherine spent tens of thousands of roubles on purchasing the libraries of Voltaire, Diderot, D'Alembert, and others. ■ This is also how female education – something totally new for Russia – emerged. Its foundation was laid in 1764 with the creation of the Smolny Institute where 200 daughters of the nobility studied for twelve years, from the age of 6 to 18. ■ Catherine's particular passion was collecting. She bought everything: paintings, graphic art, sculpture, books, coins, porcelain, precious stones, gold and silver articles, even minerals. The ultimate result of the Empress's enthusiasms was the Hermitage, one of the greatest art museums in the world. ■ The interest taken in art by high society also stimulated the development of a national artistic school. Names like Antropov, Rokotov, Levitsky, and Borovikovsky still today immediately call to mind the remarkable works of Russian painting produced in the second half of the eighteenth century. ■ In Catherine's Russia the ideas of the Enlightenment were not restricted to propaganda and the blind application of European experience to Russian life. They gave a definite impetus to the development of a national self-awareness. Kliuchevsky wrote: "Catherine did not give the people freedom and enlightenment, because such things are not given by decree, but are acquired through development and awareness, are earned by personal labor, and not received for nothing like alms. […] During her reign Russian society sensed for the first time its international strength; she revealed it to itself."

EMPRESS CATHERINE II IN THE PARK AT TSARSKOYE SELO

*1827*
*Engraving by Nikolai Utkin from the original by Vladimir*
*Borovikovsky*
*64 x 47*

Of all her country residences, Catherine II loved Tsarskoye Selo the
best and spent almost every summer here. Vladimir Borovikovsky
painted the elderly Empress in 1791 during a stroll in the park with
her favorite dog.
Catherine points to the Kagul Obelisk set up not far from the palace
in commemoration of the Russian army's victory on the Kagul River
during the war with Turkey in 1768–74.

"MIRROR". 1775. BY AN UNKNOWN WORKSHOP
*Silver-plated copper, oval plates made of silver*

*Peter I's three decrees are engraved on the plates:*
*1. On Protection of Civil Rights (April 17, 1722)*
*2. On Behavior in Court (January 21. 1724)*
*3. On State Regulations and Their Importance (January 22, 1724)*
*Height 90*

THE UNVEILING OF THE MONUMENT TO PETER I ON
SENATE SQUARE

*1782*
*Engraving by A. Mylnikov from a drawing by A. Davydov*
*51.8 x 78.6*

The ceremonial inauguration of the monument took place in St. Petersburg on the 100th anniversary of Peter's accession to the throne. On August 7, 1782, in the presence of the reigning Tsarina, Empress Catherine II, and foreign ambassadors, the monument was unveiled to the accompaniment of gunfire. The statue was created by Etienne-Maurice Falconet. On the granite rock of the pedestal is the Latin inscription, *Petro Primo Catharina Secunda MDCCLXXXII.* "The Bronze Horseman," as Alexander Pushkin called the statue, is one of the largest monuments in the city.

EMBLEM OF ST. PETERSBURG

*1785*
*Watercolor. Detail of a page from the Charter of Catherine II*

*On the field of a French escutcheon of red color are the nautical symbols of the city, the gilt anchor and grapnel, and an article of the royal regalia – the gilt scepter. Officially the emblem of St. Petersburg was established by Catherine II.*

CHARTER GRANTED TO THE CITIZENS OF ST. PETERSBURG BY CATHERINE II (IN FACT, THE STATUTE OF THE CITY)

*1785*
*The charter bears the signature of Catherine II and Vice-Chancellor Ivan Ostermann*

*This is the original manuscript of 41 parchment leaves (the text is both handwritten and printed). Pictures and ornamental designs are in watercolors. Fixed to a tasseled cord is the wax seal with the State Emblem of Russia, contained in a gilt case.*
*43 x 21*

LID OF THE CASKET WHICH CONTAINED THE CHARTER OF THE CITY OF ST. PETERSBURG

*Made at the Academy of Arts Foundry in St. Petersburg in the late 18th century*
*Ormolu. 70 x 64 x 150*

*At the obelisk are the figures of Catherine II and a nobleman bowing before her in gratitude. On the obelisk, framed by a wreath is the monogram of Catherine II and below, on the four sides, are inscriptions in Russian, French, English, and German, quoting from the Charter:*

*"The City Council should take care:*
FIRST, TO PROCURE EVERY METHOD FOR PROVIDING THE INHABITANTS OF THE TOWN. THE MEANS OF GANING THEIR SUBSISTANCE, AND MAINTENANCE.

SECONDLY, TO PRESERVE THE TOWN FROM MISUNDERSTANDINGS OR LAW SUITS WHICH MAY ARISE WITH THE NEIGHBOURING TOWNS AND VILLAGES.

THIRDLY, TO MAIN TAIN, PEACE, TRANQUI1ITY AND A COOD UNDERSTANDING AMONGST THE INHABITANTS.

FOURTHLY, TO PREVENT EVERY EVIL WHICH IS AGAINST COOD ORDER, AND DECENCY, LEAVING WHAT CONCERNS THE POLICE TO THOSE PERSONS AND PLACES APPOINTED FOR THAT PURPOSE.

FIFTHLY, BY PROPER ATTENTION: GOOD FAITH, AND EVERY METHOD TO ENCOURAGE THE BRINGING TO MARKETT, ALL THE NECESSARY ARTICLES FOR THE USE, AND ADVANTAGE OF THE CITIZENS.

SIXTHLY, TO PAY STRICT ATTENTION TO THE SOLIDITY OF ALL PUBLICK BUILDINGS, APPERTANING TO THE TOWN, AND TO BUILD SUCH AS ARE NECESSARY, APPOINTING THE PROPER PLACES FOR PUBLICK MARKETTS, WHARFS, WARE HOUSES, MAGAZINES AND CA. AND SUCH AS ARE ABSOLUTELY WANTING FOR THE USE AND ADVANTAGE OF THE INHABITANTS.

SEVENTHLY, TO ENDEAVOUR, TO ENCREASE THE TOWN SUNDS FOR ITS BENEFIT, AND THE ENLARGING UNDERTAKINGS ORDERED BY THE COURT ESTABLISHED FOR THE PUBLICK BENEFIT.

EIGTHLY, TO EXPLAIN DOUBTFULL, AND MISUNDER STOOD REGULATIONS, MADE FOR THE HANDICRAFTSMEN TRADESMEN AND MERCHANTS.'

*The casket with the Charter was kept in the City Duma on Nevsky Prospekt.*

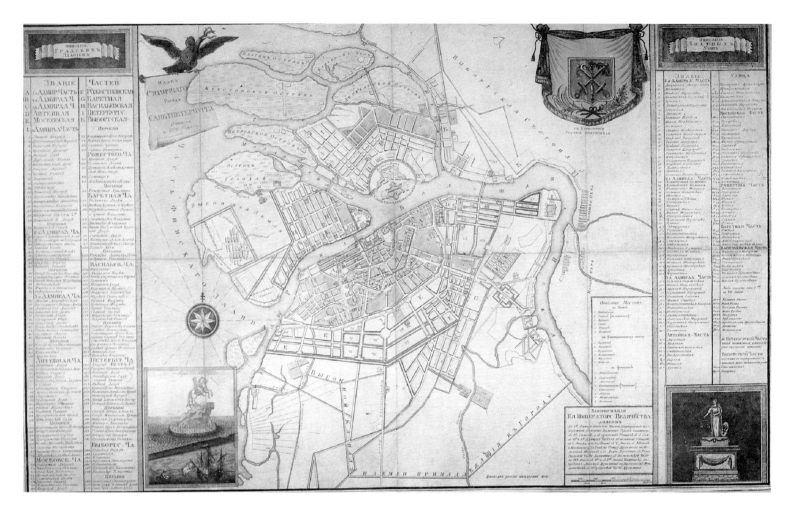

PLAN OF ST. PETERSBURG IN 1792

*Engraving tinted with watercolor*
*59 x 97*

*During the reign of Catherine II, town-building was conducted on a large scale. St. Petersburg was provided with new services and utilities, and underwent considerable reconstruction. Many industrial enterprises were moved beyond its limits, the southern border of the city was expanded, and a new plan for the Petersburg Side was drawn up. Canal and river embankments were constructed and new housing blocks created in the Admiralty district. Most of the plans for the construction of the capital, conceived under Catherine, were realized at the end of Alexander I's reign.*

THE UPPER EMBANKMENT IN ST. PETERSBURG
*1778*
*Engraving tinted with watercolor by Jacques Philippe Lebas from a painting by Jean Baptiste Le Prince*
*47.5 x 72.8*

*The epoch of Catherine II was a golden age for Petersburg construction. During her reign the foundations were laid of the Petersburg so admired by later poets, writers and artists. This engraving from Le Prince's original dates from the very beginning of Catherine's reign. In the 18th century, the riverbank was called the Upper Embankment (now the Palace Embankment). The city panorama shows the palace of the French ambassador, Marquis de L'Hopital. Opposite, on the small island, is the St. Petersburg Fortress (later renamed Peter and Paul Fortress). The spire of the Peter and Paul Cathedral became the key architectural feature in the city's panorama; its height is 122 meters. From the 18th century on, the cathedral was used as the burial place of the Russian emperors.*

ST. NICHOLAS'S CATHEDRAL
*1843*
*Lithograph by Andre Durand*
*53.5 x 43*

*In 1753, the foundation for a naval regimental church in stone was laid to plans by architect Sabbas Chevakinsky. Between 1756 and 1758, a four-tiered bell-tower was erected separate from the cathedral. The two-story cathedral was consecrated in 1762 in the presence of Catherine II. In memory of ten victories won by the Russian fleet, the Empress presented ten icons in gold mounts to the cathedral. A particle of the relics of the saint and miracle-worker Nicholas together with a particle of the relics of St. Alexander, a martyr of the 1st century, are preserved here. The relics were brought from Naples by Empress Alexandra Fedorovna, wife of Nicholas I, and transferred to the cathedral in 1847. The cathedral is commonly known as the Cathedral of St. Nicholas of the Sea.*

HEADDRESS (MITER) OF A BISHOP.

*Late 18th century. Silver, jewels. Height 20.*

SACERDOTAL ROBE (CHASUBLE) OF A DEACON AT THE
PETER AND PAUL CATHEDRAL.

*Late 18th century. Monastic work: gold brocade, galloon, velvet, silk
and other materials. Height 150.*

ICON OF ST. NICHOLAS, ARCHBISHOP OF MYRA, A GREAT
CHRISTIAN SAINT AND MIRACLE-WORKER PARTICULARLY
REVERED AND LOVED IN RUSSIA

*Painting on panel, 1910. Silver setting, 1850. 53 x 65*

*The icon belonged to the Peter and Paul Cathedral.*

*Vue de Boutiques russes au perspectif de Newsk,
avec la maison de Ville à S. Petersbourg.*

NEVSKY PROSPEKT BY THE GOSTINY DVOR TRADING
ARCADE

*First quarter of the 19th century
Engraving tinted with watercolor by Benjamin Paterssen
48.5 x 65.5*

*The corner of Nevsky Prospekt and Sadovaya Street. The
monumental Gostiny Dvor arcade was erected in 1785 to a design by
Vallin de la Mothe. Gostiny Dvor, the major trading center in St.
Petersburg, where only manufactured goods were sold.*

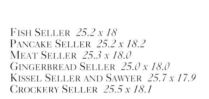

FISH SELLER  *25.2 x 18*
PANCAKE SELLER  *25.2 x 18.2*
MEAT SELLER  *25.3 x 18.0*
GINGERBREAD SELLER  *25.0 x 18.0*
KISSEL SELLER AND SAWYER  *25.7 x 17.9*
CROCKERY SELLER  *25.5 x 18.1*

*Engravings tinted with watercolor from a series by the German artists Christian Gottfried Heinrich Geißler and Christian Gotthelf Schünberg, published in 1801–03 and dedicated to Petersburg artisans and pedlars. The artists lived in St. Petersburg and studied the life of the common people. This series of engravings enjoyed great popularity and was re-issued several times.*

Съ Петербургскій Императорскій Ассигнаціонный банкъ

La Banc Imperial
à S. Petersbourg

THE ISSUE BANK

*Late 18th – early 19th century*
*Engraving tinted with watercolor*
*47 x 64.5*

*The bank was established for issuing bank notes and their exchange*
*for copper, silver and gold coins. The building was erected by*
*Giacomo Quarenghi during the reign of Catherine II. From 1799 to*
*1805, when the Mint was being re-equipped, coins were minted here.*

# *Paul I*

REIGNED

*1 7 9 6*  *1 8 0 1*

With the succession of Paul I the age of Catherine the Great came to an abrupt end. The throne was now occupied by a man brought up in that era, but harboring a passionate hatred for it. ■ The alienation which had grown up between mother and son from the first years of Paul's life, mistrust, secret surveillance, the abuse of the Empress's favorites all left their mark on the character of the future Emperor, making him embittered and suspicious. ■ In his long years of voluntary seclusion on the Gatchina estate which his mother had given him in 1783, Paul nurtured his own plans for the transformation of Russia, plans which were marked on his accession by the immediate destruction of all existing orders. ■ Paul's reign began with the coronation of the remains of his father Peter III, which were brought from the Alexander Nevsky Monastery to the Winter Palace, and from there, together with Catherine's coffin, to the Peter and Paul Cathedral. ■ Paul opposed the advances of the revolutionary French in Europe and when Napoleon captured the island of Malta he took the Knights of Malta under his protection and declared himself their grand master. In St. Petersburg a Catholic chapel was built for the order by Giacomo Quarenghi just off Nevsky Prospekt, close to the Gostiny Dvor trading arcade. ■ Even those of his actions which were objectively positive, such as the 1797 law on succession which put an end to intrigues around the throne, were motivated more by personal than by political considerations. ■ In the very first days of the new reign those free-thinkers condemned by Catherine II were brought back from their fortress prisons or places of exile. But at the same time the Peter and Paul Fortress was being filled up with new prisoners, chiefly army officers. ■ Wishing to show himself as a "people's tsar," Paul slightly improved the condition of the peasantry, but on the other hand he gave more than 500,000 state peasants as serfs to various nobles. ■ The basic provisions of the Charters to the Nobility and to the Cities were canceled, their self-administration in effect done away with and replaced by a bureaucratic apparatus. And, most importantly, the personal immunity of the nobility and distinguished citizens was removed. By a decree of 1797 corporal punishment for serious crimes was extended to all classes. ■ In the army a struggle against em-

**EMPEROR PAUL I**

*19th century*
*By an unknown artist*
*Oil on canvas*
*43.5 x 32*

*Paul is shown wearing the uniform of a general in the Preobrazhensky Regiment with the Order of St. Anne in diamonds, the cross of the Commander of the Knights of Malta and the Star of the Order of St. Andrew the First-Called.*

bezzlement, the creation of soldiers' schools and homes for children orphaned by war was combined with blind adulation of King Frederick II of Prussia. Prussian army regulations were introduced in Russia together with the Prussian uniform which proved most unsuitable for local conditions. The great military commander Alexander Suvorov fell into disgrace. Officers were dismissed from the guards and the ordinary army and those appointed in their places were both ignorant and incompetent. ■ The Emperor equated order in the state with strict discipline which embraced all aspects of social life and was taken to absurd lengths. Police surveillance reigned in the country; officer-*pristavs* attended balls and parties. Paul's subjects were forbidden to use the words "citizen" or "fatherland." Strict censorship was in operation. In 1800, the import of foreign books and sheet music was completely suspended. A ban on free movement out of the country came into force; young people were prevented from going abroad to study. A decree was published banning the wearing of round hats, high boots and lace-up shoes. Nobody was permitted to wear sidewhiskers, women were forbidden to wear blue skirts with white blouses and so on. ■ Life in St. Petersburg became like that in a barracks. As a contemporary recollected: "St. Petersburg ceased to resemble a modern capital, taking on the dreary appearance of a small German town in the eighteenth century." ■ On Paul's orders sentry-boxes were set up on the city streets painted in Prussian colors, white and black. It was forbidden to drive or ride quickly around the city. After eight in the evening, when the Emperor went to bed, the lights were supposed to be put out in all the houses of St. Petersburg. ■ In 1797, at Paul's command, on the site of Empress Elizabeth's Summer Palace in the center of the capital, the foundations were laid for the St. Michael's Castle which was destined to become the Emperor's last residence. Construction work continued on it day and night. It was enclosed on all four sides by canals and cannon stood by the drawbridges over them. Prey to suspicion and distrust, Paul hoped that the castle would become an inaccessible fortress for his enemies. But with every passing day society nurtured increasing discontent toward the Emperor which extended to his close retinue and even members of the royal family who lived in constant fear as their fate too depended on the mood of the monarch. ■ Paul's suspiciousness and whims made everyone feel they were walking a tightrope and left him completely isolated. In a fit of rage he banished the last people loyal to him – Counts Fedor Rostopchin and Alexei Arakcheyev – from St. Petersburg, and so signed his own death warrant.

On the night of 11 March 1801, he was murdered by guards officers in the bedchamber of St. Michael's Castle. ■ In the history of the country and its capital a new era had begun.

FIREWORKS MARKING THE MARRIAGE OF TSESAREVICH
PAVEL PETROVICH

*1773*
*Engraving by Christoph Melchior Roth*
*49 x 56*

*In the fall of 1773 St. Petersburg celebrated the marriage of Grand
Duke Pavel Petrovich (the future Emperor Paul I) and Grand
Duchess Natalia Alexeyevna, Princess of Hesse-Darmstadt. The
fireworks portrayed here were designed by Jacob Stehlin. The
engraving depicts the first tableau, "The Temple of Bliss with a
Sacrificial Altar."*

ИМПЕРАТОРСКОЙ ДВОРЕЦЪ | PALAIS IMPERIAL

ВЪ ГАТЧИНѢ | DE GATCHINA

GATCHINA PALACE FROM THE PARADE-GROUND

*Mid 19th century*
*Lithograph of C. Schultz from a drawing by Joseph Charlemagne*
*37.5 x 50*

*Not far from St. Petersburg, on the small estate of Gatchina, a palace
was built by the Italian architect Antonio Rinaldi for Catherine II's
favorite, Count Grigory Orlov. Construction, begun in 1766,
continued for almost fifteen years. After Orlov's death in 1783,
Catherine gave Gatchina to her son, Grand Duke Pavel Petrovich.
After he ascended the throne as Paul I in 1796, the palace was
reconstructed by the architect Vincenzo Brenna.
In the middle of the 19th century, the palace was again rebuilt and on
the parade-ground a monument to Paul I was set up. In the 1880s,
Emperor Alexander III chose Gatchina as his permanent residence.*

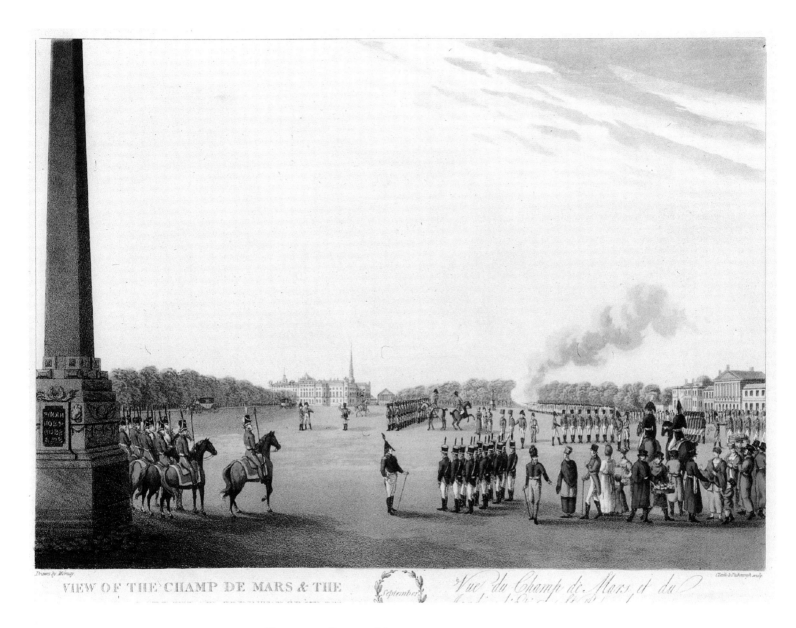

VIEW OF THE CHAMP DE MARS & THE    *September*    *Vue du Champ de Mars, et du*

VIEW OF THE FIELD OF MARS

*1815*
*Engraving by M. Dubourgh and John H. Clark from a drawing by*
*Mornay*
*30.5 x 46*

*Military exercises, reviews and parades took place on the Field of
Mars next to the Summer Gardens. In the foreground is the obelisk set
up in 1799 to commemorate the victories of Field Marshal Pyotr
Rumyantsev in the Russian-Turkish wars. Left, in the background is
St. Michael's Castle, built by 1800 for Emperor Paul I. He lived
there for only forty days and was killed in his own bedchamber.*

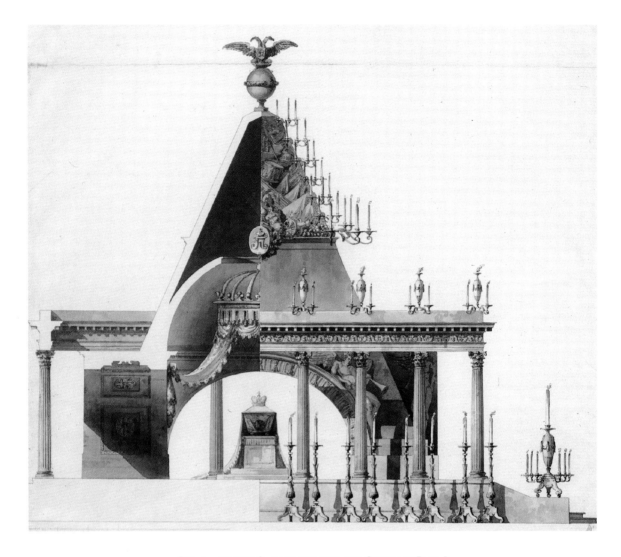

DESIGN FOR THE CATAFALQUE OVER THE COFFIN OF PAUL I

*1801*
*Draft by Vincenzo Brenna*
*India ink and watercolor*
*45 x 51.5*

*The obsequies for the Emperor ended in the Peter and Paul Cathedral, the burial place of the Russian tsars. Court architects and artists were invited to design decorations for the funeral ceremony, the entrance to the cathedral and the catafalque.*

# Alexander I

REIGNED

### 1 8 0 1 — 1 8 2 5

The death of Paul I and succession of his son was received with rejoicing in St. Petersburg society. Yet Alexander's ascent to the throne was bound up with the murder of his father. Today no historian would venture to say that Alexander I knew nothing of the brewing conspiracy. Indeed, he not only knew, but took part in the preparations as was proved by previously unknown evidence discovered in the royal family archives by the famous historian Grand Duke Nikolai Mikhailovich, a grandson of Nicholas I. ■ Having come to the throne as the eighteenth century gave way to the nineteenth, the twenty-three-year-old Alexander I felt the influence of both centuries and himself became the embodiment of a whole era not only in Russian, but in European history. ■ Within hours of Paul I's murder the new Emperor left St. Michael's Castle and moved to the Winter Palace, the permanent residence of the Russian rulers. That same night the manifesto on Alexander's accession to the throne was compiled. It included a promise to rule "according to the laws and heart of Catherine II," which meant the abandonment of Paul's policy. ■ The first period of his reign is characterized by the fact that the Emperor, brought up on the ideas of the "Jacobin and republican" LaHarpe, was disturbed about Russia's well-being and dreamed of giving the country a constitution. He frequently said that the chief shortcoming of power was "the arbitrariness of our rule." To dispose of this required the adoption of

**EMPEROR ALEXANDER I**

*Early 19th century*
*By an unknown artist*
*Oil on canvas*
*79 x 64*

*Alexander I is portrayed wearing a general's full-dress uniform with the ribbon of the Order of St. Andrew the First-Called and an ermine mantle.*

fundamental laws of which there were hardly any in Russia. ■ From the earliest steps he took Alexander was not only considering constitutional reform, but also preparing some social and economic changes. His chief aide in this was Mikhail Speransky, who occupied a prominent place among the Tsar's retinue. With his involvement a number of laws were adopted, including one on the transformation of the colleges dating back to Peter I's time into ministries – an attempt to reform the central government. ■ In 1801, a decree issued by the Emperor permitted members of all free classes to acquire real estate outside the towns, i.e. land without peasants. This right was now available to the lower middle classes, state peasants and merchants, thus breaking in effect the nobility's age-old monopoly of the right to hold land as personal property.

In 1803, the "Law Concerning the Free Agriculturists" was published which permitted landowners to free peasants together with land – only, of course, if they were so minded. Many of the reforms which the Emperor intended to bring about with Speransky's help were never carried out. Of the three branches of government – the executive, legislative and judiciary – he managed to reform only the first two, while the third remained unaltered. ■ The implementation of domestic changes was hindered by the war which Russia waged against France, first in alliance with Austria in 1805, then with Prussia in 1806–07. Defeat in the war and the conclusion of the Peace of Tilsit in 1807 and subsequently of a Franco-Russian alliance was economically damaging, and forced compliance with the continental blockade caused serious financial losses. St. Petersburg society held Alexander I to be personally responsible. The situation was open to correction by the financial reform which Speransky proposed, based on two elements – stopping the issue of new bank notes and the raising of all taxes. This reform was especially unpopular since it affected the economic interests of all classes of society. As a result Speransky had to resign and was then sent into exile. That was the end of the political career of one of the most educated and talented men in Russia whose activities as a statesman are an inseparable element of Alexander I's era. ■ This took place in 1812 just three months before Napoleon began his war against Russia, the conflict that has gone down in Russian history as the "Patriotic War." The shocks of the war and subsequent events radically changed the Emperor's domestic policy. In the second part of his reign he no longer even thought of sweeping reforms, feeling disillusioned with his own former political ideals. ■ Having defeated Napoleon in 1814 Alexander I returned to Russia exhausted from the upheavals which even turned his hair gray. Russia's victory over Napoleon was regarded in Western Europe as the defeat of revolutionary France and Alexander was looked on as the defender of lawful order. The guarantee of that order was the Holy Alliance created by Austria, Prussia and Russia to fight against the spread of seditious ideas in Europe. Consequently the main emphasis in Alexander's policy in the postwar years was on international relations, and their conservative character carried over into Russian domestic politics as well. ■ The rise of patriotism in Russian society produced by the War of 1812 promoted a revival of ideas of liberation and the formation of secret societies which set themselves the goal of overturning the existing order and establishing constitutional government in the country. ■ The great historical disturbances of Alexander I's reign found reflection in the appearance of the capital. Majestic architectural creations designed by Russians and foreigners took their place on the central squares and streets of St. Petersburg. ■ The city duma, although still subordinate to the governor's rule, was granted greater independence. In order to check that the inhabitants of St. Petersburg were fulfilling their duties toward the municipal authority, a Committee for the Settlement of Municipal Obligations was set up in 1802, while in 1816 a Committee for Constructions and Hydraulic Works was established. This latter body concerned itself not only with the construction of buildings, but also with the maintenance of the city. At the beginning of the nineteenth century the Obvodny (Bypass) Canal was started; in the period from 1806 to 1816 the wooden bridges across the Moika River were replaced by iron ones clad in stone (the Police, Red and Potseluyev Bridges) and in 1820 metal chain bridges were constructed across the Fontanka (the Pantaleon and Egyptian Bridges). From 1817 sidewalks began to be laid along all the paved streets in the city. Measures were taken against fires, but the greatest evil for the city was flooding. The most damaging instance was the flood of 1824. Alexander I's reign also saw the start of the construction of urban public parks. ■ St. Petersburg possessed the largest seaport in Europe. The greater part of Russia's trade, both domestic and with Western Europe was conducted through the city. ■ Alexander I's almost twenty-five-year reign ended with his sudden death on 19 November 1825 in the southern Russian town of Taganrog. The unexpectedness of this event gave rise to legends, the most widespread of which claimed that the Tsar had not in fact died but hidden and was now living in Siberia in the guise of a wanderer named Fedor Kuzmich. His grave in the Peter and Paul Cathedral in St. Petersburg, the burial place of the Russian emperors, was said to contain the remains of a common soldier. These rumors were given credibility by the fact that the late Emperor's body was conveyed to St. Petersburg in great haste and, contrary to Russian tradition, the coffin was not opened before or during the funeral. ■ The desire which the Emperor expressed in his youth to give up the throne and lead a solitary life, the memory of his father's murder which constantly haunted him, and also the profound religiosity which characterized the last years of his life all went to develop a mystical strain in Alexander's soul which has given historians cause to believe the story about the itinerant Fedor Kuzmich. Grand Duke Alexander Mikhailovich also wrote on this topic in his memoirs: "… the Tsar, exhausted by the long drawn-out wars with Napoleon and having lost all faith in his German, English and Austrian allies, loved to live for months at a time in the provincial remoteness of the Taganrog palace with his sad, beautiful wife, who mourned her long years of childlessness, and he incessantly read the words of Ecclesiasticus in the Bible.

DESK SET OF EMPEROR ALEXANDER I. EARLY 19TH CENTURY

*Ormolu. 28 x 19 x 27.5*

*This set was used by Alexander I when signing the Treaty of Tilsit with Napoleon in 1807 on a raft anchored in the River Neman. The set was kept in the Ministry of Foreign Affairs on Palace Square, St. Petersburg.*

BREASTPLATE FROM ALEXANDER I'S UNIFORM

*First quarter, 19th century*
*Copper enriched with gilding and engraving. 22.5 x 24*

*The inscription on the breastplate reads: The Life-Guards Preobrazhensky Regiment uniform of his Late Majesty Emperor Alexander I.*

THE STUDY OF ALEXANDER I IN THE WINTER PALACE
*1830s*

*By Lavr Plakhov (?)*
*Oil on canvas*
*48 x 66*

*Emperor Alexander I's study was located in the northwestern part of the Winter Palace. The architectural decoration in the austere classical style was executed by the architect Vasily Stasov in 1819.*

*Видъ Трiумфальныхъ воротъ воздвигнутыхъ въ честь Россiйской Императорской Гвардiи, и торжественное ея въ шествiе въ Санктпетербургъ въ Iюле 31го 1814 года.*

*Vue de l'arc Triomphal erigé à l'honneur de la garde Imperiale Russe, et son entrée à St Petersbourg, en Juillet 31. 1814.*

## THE NARVA TRIUMPHAL GATE

*1815*
*Engraving tinted with watercolor*
*53 x 70.5*

The Narva Triumphal Gate was built to commemorate the victory over Napoleon I in the War of 1812 (architect Giacomo Quarenghi, sculptor Ivan Terebenev).
After receiving the news that Russian forces had entered Paris in the spring of 1814, preparations were begun for the ceremonial meeting of the victorious troops in St. Petersburg. Later the dilapidated original wooden gate was dismantled. Between 1827 and 1834 a gate of brick with copper facing was constructed to plans by Vasily Stasov.

## THE FLOOD OF 1824 IN ST. PETERSBURG

*First quarter of the 19th century*
*Engraving*
*23.5 x 36.5*

Floods were a natural hazard in St. Petersburg. Throughout its history there have been more than sixty floods. The greatest occurred in November 1824 when the Neva waters rose 4.1 meters, submerging a large part of the city. Thousands of townspeople perished and the lowest regions of St. Petersburg were destroyed. This tragic event is the subject of Alexander Pushkin's poem, the Bronze Horseman.

**PARADE IN FRONT OF THE WINTER PALACE**

*First quarter of the 19th century*
*Engraving tinted with watercolor*
*44 x 68*

As St. Petersburg was also the military capital, the Guards regiments were quartered here. In the 1820s, of every ten inhabitants, one was a member of the Guards. On festive occasions, parades and guard reviews were held on Palace Square. Depicted in the center is Emperor Alexander I wearing a red full-dress uniform.

MODELS FOR THE STATUES OF MIKHAIL KUTUZOV AND
MIKHAIL BARCLAY DE TOLLY, THE RUSSIAN COMMANDERS
IN THE WAR OF 1812 WITH NAPOLEON

*1831–32. By Boris Orlovsky*
*Chased patinated bronze. 14 x 16 x 47 and 15 x 16 x 47*

OUR LADY OF KAZAN CATHEDRAL ON NEVSKY PROSPEKT

*First quarter of the 19th century*
*Engraving tinted with watercolor by Benjamin Paterssen*
*48 x 65.5*

*The cathedral is named after the miracle-working icon of Our Lady
of Kazan – the protectress of the Imperial House of Romanov –
which was kept here. In 1800, Paul I commissioned a design from the
architect Andrei Voronikhin and in 1801, under Alexander I, the
foundation of the capital's main cathedral was laid. Kept in the
cathedral were captured French colors, the staff of the French
marshal Davout, and keys to the fortresses and cities of Western
Europe taken by Russian troops during the war against Napoleon.
One of the heroes of the war, the Commander-in-Chief of the Russian
army, Field Marshal Mikhail Kutuzov, is buried here. The silver
iconostasis of the Kazan Cathedral was executed to the design of the
architect Konstantin Thon. In the 1920s, all the church plate of
precious metals and the iconostasis were removed and the cathedral
was converted into an anti-religious museum.*

INTERIOR OF OUR LADY OF KAZAN CATHEDRAL
*1840s–50s*
*Lithograph tinted with watercolor*
*44 x 60.5*

Видъ С.П. Бургскаго главнаго Адмиралтейства.                     Vue de l' Amirauté à S.t Petersbourg.

### THE ADMIRALTY

*1814*
*Engraving tinted with watercolor*
*41 x 59*

The Admiralty was a large shipyard dating back to the Petrine era.
Between 1806 and 1823 it was reconstructed in the classical style by
Adrian Zakharov. The tower with a spire is one of the dominant
features of the city's skyline. The boulevard laid out in front of the
Admiralty in 1817 was a fashionable place for promenades.

### THE SPIT OF VASILYEVSKY ISLAND

*1820s*
*Engraving tinted with watercolor by I. Chesky from a drawing by M.*
*Shatoshnikov*
*55 x 81*

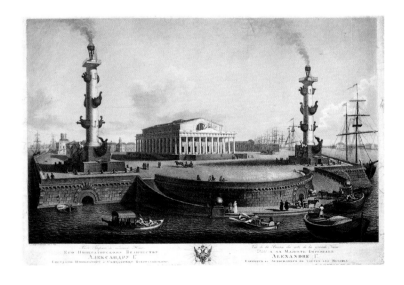

The engraving shows the Spit of Vasilyevsky Island where the Neva
River divides into the Great and Small Nevas. In the early 19th
century Adrian Zakharov worked out a general plan for the
development of the Spit and Thomas de Thomon created a grandiose
architectural ensemble. The man-made embankment serves as a base
for the monumental Exchange building reminiscent of an ancient
temple. The rostral columns, decorated with ship's prows and
extolling Russia's naval glory, served as lighthouses since a maritime
port was located here in the first half of the 19th century

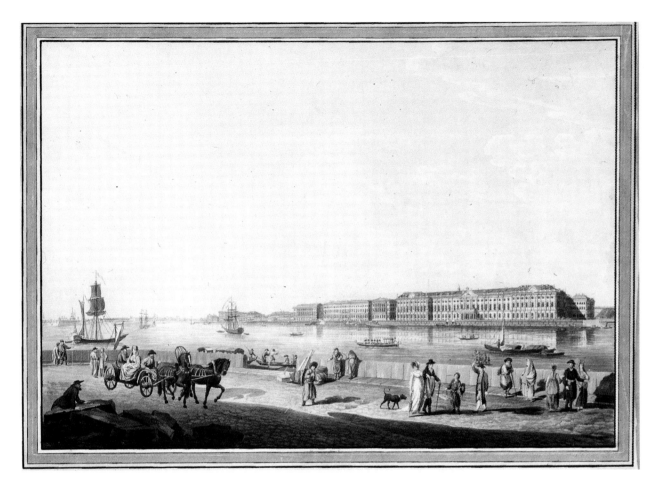

THE PALACE EMBANKMENT AND THE WINTER PALACE

*Early 19th century*
*Engraving tinted with watercolor by Benjamin Paterssen*
*44 x 60.5*

*From right to left: the Winter Palace, residence of the Russian tsars in St. Petersburg, designed in the Baroque style by Bartolomeo Francesco Rastrelli in the middle of the 18th century; next to it is the Small Hermitage built in the classical style in 1775 by Jean-Baptiste Vallin de la Mothe and the Old Hermitage (1771–87) designed by Yuri Velten. The arched passageway from the Old Hermitage to the Hermitage Theater is by the outstanding Petersburg architect Giacomo Quarenghi. Today all these buildings belong to the Hermitage Museum*

VUE DU MILIEU DU GRAND PONT, DE LA NEWA ET DE St PÉTERSBOURG.

VIEW UP THE NEVA FROM ST. ISAAC'S BRIDGE

*1812*
*Engraving tinted with watercolor by M. Dubourg*
*50 x 64*

*In the foreground is the pontoon St. Isaac's Bridge, connecting Vasilyevsky Island with the Admiralty. During Peter I's lifetime bridges across the Neva were not built. In the winter people walked and rode on the frozen Neva while in the summer they crossed the river in boats. In 1727, the first bridge was opened across the Neva opposite the Church of St. Isaac of Dalmatia, hence the bridge's name. Anchored pontoons with plank flooring could also be drawn aside to allow the passage of ships.*

THE KAMENNOOSTROVSKY PALACE

*1810s*
*Gouache by Johann Wilhelm Barth*
*36 x 51.5*

*One of the islands of the Neva delta, Kamenny (Stone) Island was given by Catherine II in 1765 to her son, Grand Duke Pavel Petrovich (the future Emperor Paul I). Construction of the Kamennoostrovsky Palace began in the spring of 1776. After the palace revolution of 1801 and Alexander I's accession to the throne, Kamennoostrovsky Palace became the favorite residence of the new emperor. A seven-span wooden bridge which led to the island was built between 1811 and 1813 to the design of engineer Augustin Betancourt.*

PLATE WITH A VIEW OF THE KAMENNOOSTROVSKY PALACE (BELONGING TO EMPEROR ALEXANDER I)
*1810s–20s*

*Imperial Porcelain Factory*
*Porcelain, printing, tinting, gilding*
*Diameter 23.5*

*The miniature was engraved by Ivan Chesky from the original by Semyon Shchedrin*
*In 1814, printing, a rare technique in those days, was introduced for the decoration of porcelain at the Imperial Porcelain Factory. Views of St. Petersburg and its suburbs were the most popular subjects. Articles with printed designs by this factory are rare both in museums and in private collections.*

MUG WITH A VIEW OF THE ANICHKOV PALACE AND ALEXANDRINSKY THEATER ON NEVSKY PROSPEKT

*1830s*
*Imperial Porcelain Factory*
*Porcelain, overglaze painting, polished and matt gilding*
*Height 25*

*Very often representations of Nevsky Prospekt were based on the lithographed watercolors of Vasily Sadovnikov showing both sides of the street from the Admiralty to the Anichkov Palace in minute detail.*

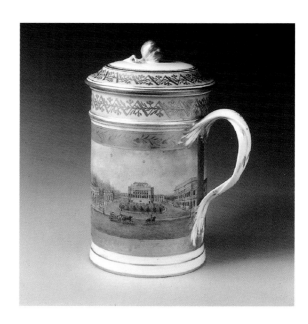

PLATE WITH A VIEW OF THE TAURIDA PALACE BUILT FOR
PRINCE GRIGORY POTEMKIN, A FAVORITE OF CATHERINE II

*1810s–20s*
*From the watercolor by Semyon Shchedrin*
*Imperial Porcelain Factory*
*Porcelain, printing, tinting, gilding*
*Diameter 23.5*

*After Potemkin's death, the palace passed to the State and was used
for gala occasions. Between 1904 and 1917 sessions of the State
Duma were held in this palace.*

CUP AND SAUCER WITH A VIEW OF PAUL I'S PALACE, BUILT
BY CATHERINE II IN 1777–78 FOR HER SON PAUL

*1820s*
*Batenin's Factory*
*Porcelain, overglaze painting, polished and matt gilding*
*Height of cup 13.2, Diameter of saucer 17.4*

*In the early 19th century private factories began to play an
important role in the production of porcelain in Russia. Among these,
the Batenin Factory in St. Petersburg occupied a prominent place.
Vases, services and presentation cups with views of St. Petersburg
and its suburbs were in great demand. Presentation cups and mugs
were made in different sizes and models.*

CUP AND SAUCER WITH A VIEW OF VASILYEVSKY ISLAND
AND THE STOCK EXCHANGE, WHERE THE ST. PETERSBURG
HARBOR WAS LOCATED AT THAT TIME

*First third, 19th century*
*Francis Gardner's Factory (the first Russian private enterprise in
porcelain industry founded in 1766 by the English merchant Francis
Gardner)*
*Porcelain, overglaze painting, polished and matt gilding*
*Height of cup 9.2. Diameter of saucer 12.8*

TOBOGGANING ON THE NEVA
*1817*

*Lithograph tinted with watercolor by Armand Gustave Houbigant*
*29 x 45*

*Tobogganing was a favorite winter pastime of St. Petersburg citizens. The hills, erected on the ice of the Neva, on squares and boulevards, were built of wood, decorated with fir trees and brightly adorned with flags.*

ICE SKATING ON THE NEVA

*First quarter of the 19th century*
*Engraving tinted with watercolor by Emelyan Karneyev*
*29.7 x 36*

*The favorite winter amusement of the young nobility was skating on the Neva. This pursuit drew a crowd of idlers from the common people and attracted pedlars selling sheeten, a popular Russia drink composed of hot water, honey and spices.*

*Jeu du Katcheli et foire Russe*

**SHOW BOOTHS AND SWINGS**

*1817*
*Lithograph tinted with watercolor by Armand Gustave Houbigant*
*29.5 x 44*

If tobogganing was the focal point of winter fêtes, during the spring festivals it was replaced with the swings, the favorite amusement of the Russian people. Swings of various kinds were an indispensable attribute of festive popular fetes, In the 18th and 19th centuries, both simple and "up-and-over" swings were used, the latter intended for lovers of a sharp sensation since the cabins, containing people and attached to the central axis, rose high above the ground. These latter swings are represented in the lithograph.

**FESTIVAL ON THE ICE OF THE NEVA OPPOSITE THE PETER AND PAUL FORTRESS**

*First quarter of the 19th century*
*Engraving*
*42.5 x 53.5*

Every year when the Neva froze, opposite the Peter and Paul Fortress Maslenitsa (Shrovetide) festivals with tobogganing hills and show booths were held.

**CELEBRATION OF TRINITY SUNDAY AT THE CHURCH OF OUR LADY OF VLADIMIR**

*1815*
*Engraving tinted with watercolor by Ivan Ivanov*
*46.8 x 65.5*

This church consecrated to Our Lady of Vladimir was built in 1769 and the bell-tower was added in 1783. The church is located on Vladimirsky Prospekt that branches off the Nevsky.

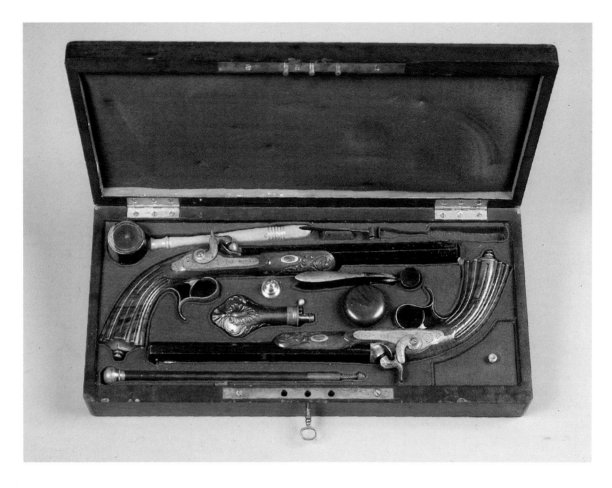

DUELLING PISTOLS

*19th century*
*Walnut, burnished steel*
*15.5 x 40 x 3.5*

*Duels first took place in Russia in the early 18th century. However, Peter I's Military Regulations already stated that participation in a duel was punishable by death*
*The Manifesto of 1787 on duels, pointing to the inadequacy of legal protection against personal abuse, nevertheless regarded the duel as premeditated murder or infliction of bodily injuries subject to punishment. A decree of 1894 legalized duels for officers only.*

# Nicholas I

REIGNED

1 8 2 5     1 8 5 5

The name of the new successor to the Russian throne, Grand Duke Nikolai Pavlovich, was not widely known at the time. Emperor Paul I had four sons and it would hardly have been possible to foresee that Alexander would die childless and that Konstantin would refuse to accept the throne. It was thus solely by chance that Alexander I's second brother, Grand Duke Nikolai Pavlovich, became emperor. He had not been as brilliantly educated as Alexander, having instead prepared himself for a more simple career in the military. Such a career interested him all the more as he was fonder of military reviews, parades and exercises than anything else. He became emperor at the age of 29 years, absolutely unprepared to assume the responsibilities of the imperial office. Nevertheless, this tall, stately and handsome man with a stern expression in his steel-gray eyes and an inflexible authoritative voice displayed determination and strength. ■ The accession of Nicholas I to the Russian throne marked the end of an interregnum. He had no intention of ascending the throne before Grand Duke Konstantin declared his refusal of it to the whole nation. Konstantin, for his part, believed that the entire matter had been stated quite clearly in 1822 in a special manifesto confirmed by Alexander I's signature and preserved in the Dormition Cathedral in Moscow. On the parcel containing this document Alexander wrote: "In the event of my death, open before initiating any other actions." In his endeavor to keep to the letter of the law, Nicholas considered it necessary to swear allegiance to Konstantin. It is likely that Konstantin's refusal to accept the throne was in the least unexpected for Nicholas. It would, in fact, be hard to imagine that this issue was not discussed within the court circles, all the more so as Konstantin had married a Polish aristocrat woman not of royal blood in 1820, and this marriage excluded him from the succession to the Russian throne. ■ The interregnum period was used by members of certain secret societies. On December 14, 1825, when the army was to swear allegiance to Nicholas, the officer conspirators – who came to be known as the Decembrists – assembled the soldiers of several regiments on Senate Square in St. Petersburg. They demanded that Nicholas abdicate and that a constitutional form of government be established. Al-

EMPEROR NICHOLAS I

*By an unknown artist, second half of the 19th century*
*Oil on canvas*
*90 x 70*

*The Emperor is shown in the uniform of the Foot Guards with stars of the Orders of St. Andrew the First-Called and St. Vladimir.*

though the uprising was suppressed, the events of December 14 left their mark upon the entire span of Nicholas I's reign. From the very beginning Nicholas made it a rule to involve himself in all the more important affairs of the state. In order to realize this policy of control, he had to significantly increase the apparatus of central government. New departments were formed and numerous commissions and committees set up. The negative side to such a growth in the imperial bureaucracy was even noted by Nicholas himself who once remarked that Russia was not ruled by the emperor, but by "four thousand stolonachal'niks" (clerks). The enlargement of the governmental apparatus eventually culminated in the establishment of His Majesty's Own Chancery. It had four departments, of which the Second Department was concerned with the codification of laws. It was headed by Mikhail Speransky, who had been brought back from exile in Siberia (he had been sent there by Alexander I as a result of political intrigues and false accusations). Speransky's main objective while in this chancery was to prepare for publication *The Code of Laws of the Russian Empire*. Published in 1883, this fifteen-volume work included the laws and regulations that had been in effect in Russia for the last 200 years. Its major significance lay in the fact that all the laws were incorporated in a single system which facilitated their execution and served as the basis for formulating new legal acts.

■ The Third Department of His Majesty's Own Chancery – the political police – acted as the autocrat's main weapon against subversion and revolution. Nicholas's internal policy was distinguished not only by the strengthening of the bureaucratic apparatus and the regulation of public and private life, but also by a policy of strict press censorship. From the 1830s on, the government under Nicholas I became increasingly reactionary.

■ This tendency was furthered by political events abroad (the bourgeois revolutions of 1830 and 1848 in Western Europe) and by those internal problems that had long demanded attention (the peasant question). During Nicholas I's entire reign this question remained unresolved, despite the fact that eight *ad hoc* committees were formed to work out a law for the emancipation of the peasantry from serfdom. The Minister of State Domains, Pavel Kiselev, even presented a final draft in 1840, but it was rejected by Nicholas for fear of infringing upon the interests of landowners. ■ The greatest failure of Nicholas's foreign policy was, of course, the Crimean War of 1854. The inactivity of the Russian fleet in the Baltic in 1854 as well as the failures of the Russian army on the Danube caused anxiety which eventually grew into irritation against Nicholas I. Among the populace of St. Petersburg this was expressed in hopes for Nicholas's abdication and even his death. ■ In the 1830s and later, the question of Russia's subsequent development was constantly brought up in discussions. Two schools of thought arose out of this discussion. The first, the Westernizers, looked to development along Western European lines. The second, the Slavophiles, focused on the historical and cultural traditions of Russia, and built their program on a recognition of the spiritual values of the Russian people. Nicholas's government used these patriotic sentiments in order to develop an ideological doctrine by which he hoped to strengthen an autocracy that was being shaken as a result of an intellectual ferment within oppositional forces. The Minister of Education, Sergei Uvarov formulated the well-known triad: Orthodoxy, Autocracy and Nationality (*narodnost* in Russian). Thus arose the policy of Official Nationality, which had a strong influence on the development of public thought, literature and art. Despite all this, however, the reign of Nicholas was marked by the brilliant flourishing of Russian culture, sciences and public thought. The center of this development was St. Petersburg. The city itself is closely associated with the work of Alexander Pushkin, Mikhail Lermontov, Nikolai Gogol, the composer Mikhail Glinka, the artists Karl Briullov, Alexander Ivanov, and the actors Mikhail Shchepkin and Alexander Martynov. The names of the mathematicians Nikolai Lobachevsky and Pafnuty Chebyshev, the chemist Nikolai Zinin, the explorer Fedor Lütke, of the Russian anatomist and surgeon Nikolai Pirogov as well as of other men of science, who lived and worked in the Russian capital, shone bright throughout both Russia and the world. ■ During Nicholas I's reign the capital, like the whole country, was irresistibly dragged into the process of capitalist development. It became evident that the intensive construction of new factories and works demanded that industrial enterprises be relocated away from the center of the capital in outlying districts. In 1833, the *Statute on the Location and Construction of Private Factories* was published in St. Petersburg. In the 1850s, approximately 350 enterprises existed in the capital. This growth in industry coupled with the wide development of trade through the ports of St. Petersburg demanded an active banking system. In the capital, the three major banks which had been founded in the 18th century – the Issue Bank, the Loan Bank and the State Commercial Bank – continued to be the sole banks in operation. It was only later that private banks began to appear on the scene. ■ This new epoch of industrial development coincided with the development of railroads. In 1837, the first railroad was opened between St. Petersburg and Tsarskoye Selo. In 1851, regular transportation by rail began between the capital and Moscow. For St. Petersburg transacted by a major waterway, the Neva River, bridges were of vital importance. It was only in 1842 that the first permanent bridge across the Neva was constructed. First called the Annunciation Bridge, it was renamed the Nikolayevsky Bridge after the emperor's death in 1855. ■ In the 1830s and 1840s, gas lights made their first appearance on the capital's streets as well as wooden sidewalks along its major roadways. At this time public transport also began to operate. The outward appearance of the city changed, too. The deliberately formal magnificence that was characteristic of Nicholas I's reign found reflection in the late classical construction of St. Petersburg. These buildings determined the look of "Nicholas's Petersburg," which is justly called "Pushkin's Petersburg." Alexander Pushkin was brought to this city in 1800 while still a child and it was here that his life tragically ended. In his works the poet often had the theme of St. Petersburg. ■ Great progress in the economic life of the capital called for changes in the municipal administration. In 1846, a new regulation was enacted in order to rejuvenate the activities of the General and Executive Dumas by endowing them with expanded rights. Following an increase in the number of members from the nobility, the latter were given far-reaching control over the activities of both dumas. The government of Nicholas I attached great importance to this development. As the center of state administration St. Petersburg had a large stratum of the gentry. Here they had wide access to high government positions while the nobility of lower and middle rank comprised a significant portion of the bureaucratic and military apparatus in the capital. ■ As the center of economic and commercial life St. Petersburg attracted industrialists, merchants, craftsmen, and many foreigners of different estates and professions. It was a multinational city. Toward the end of Nicholas I's reign it had a population of 523,721, twice that in the time of Alexander I. ■ In 1855, the thirty-year reign of Nicholas I came to an end.

He was the last of the Russian emperors who ruled the country along the feudal-serfdom line. His death likewise marked the end of a long period in the development of Russia which was now entering a new historical era. Historians and contemporaries alike have evaluated the personality and the role of Nicholas I in the history of Russia in different ways. He has often been described as the gendarme of Europe and has been called the fearless knight of absolutism. Many lionized him and many hated him. Leo Tolstoy dubbed him "Nicholas the Rod." One of the famous Russian poets, Fedor Tiutchev, a Slavophile and faithful monarchist, struck a more virulent blow when he wrote: ■ "Not God did you serve, nor Russia but only your own vanity; For all your deeds both bad and good Were but empty ghosts and falsehood. You were no tsar, but an actor." ■ As in any harsh evaluation there is much truth here and, of course, much that is exaggerated.

THE DECEMBRIST REBELLION ON SENATE SQUARE

*Copy of a watercolor by Carl Kollmann, 1825*
*40.5 x 56*

*After the death of Alexander I, when the Guards regiments were to
swear allegiance to the new Emperor Nicholas I on December 14,
1825, several units under the command of officer conspirators
attempted to seize the Winter Palace and the St. Petersburg Fortress,
and to surround the Senate. They planned to force the senators to
accept a manifesto on the overthrow of autocracy, the introduction of
democratic freedoms, the abolition of serfdom and the summoning of
a constituent assembly. The rebellious regiments that drew up on
Senate Square were dispersed by artillery fire.*

DISH DEPICTING THE BRONZE HORSEMAN, THE
EQUESTRIAN STATUE OF EMPEROR PETER I ON SENATE
SQUARE

*Second quarter, 19th century*
*Imperial Porcelain Factory*

*Porcelain, overglaze painting, polished and matt gilding*
*Diameter 40.8*

VASE WITH A VIEW OF THE KAMENNOOSTROVSKY PALACE
AND THE BRIDGE ACROSS ONE OF THE BRANCHES OF THE
NEVA

*1830s–40s*
*Russian private factory*

*Porcelain, overglaze painting, polished and matt gilding*
*Height 26.4*

VASE WITH A VIEW OF THE ALEXANDER COLUMN ON
PALACE SQUARE IN ST. PETERSBURG

*1830s–40s*
*Russian private factory*

*Porcelain, overglaze painting, polished and matt gilding*
*Height 26.4*

VIEW OF PALACE SQUARE AND THE ALEXANDER COLUMN

*1840s*
*By Rodionov*
*Oil on canvas*
*60 x 45*

*The ensemble of Palace Square, the central one in the city, was created
over a period of 150 years. Between 1819 and 1820, opposite the
Winter Palace, the semicircular building of the General Staff was
erected in the classical style to the design of Carlo Rossi. The grand
triumphal arch, crowned with the Chariot of Glory, divides this
edifice into two parts, forming the main entrance to the square. The
building housed the General Staff of the Russian army and two
ministries. In the center of the square the Alexander Column rises, a
monument to Russia's victory over Napoleon in the War of 1812.
The column was built in 1829–34 from a design by Auguste
Montferrand. The granite monolith, 47.5 meters tall, is kept secure
on the pedestal entirely by its own weight.*

*Le Quai anglais, pris du Senat - Diiigiant.*

VIEW OF THE ENGLISH EMBANKMENT FROM SENATE SQUARE

*1826*
*Lithograph*
*34.5 x 49.5*

The English Embankment, one of the city's central quays, received its name in the 18th century, since the majority of merchants, artisans and workmen living here came from England. In the foreground is the House of the Governing Senate, the supreme body of state power in Russia. On the Neva is one of the first steamships built at Ch. Bird's Mechanical Works in St. Petersburg. Regular steamer travel between St. Petersburg and Kronstadt began in 1816.

LANDING STAGE AT THE ACADEMY OF ARTS

*1841*
*Lithograph tinted with watercolor by Ferdinand Victor Perrot*
*26.5 x 44.5*

A pier was located at the granite steps of the Academy of Arts. On the Neva, and also on all the rivers and canals of the city, small boats scurried about, carrying townspeople from island to island. This tradition went back to the 18th century when, by order of Peter I, a ferry service was established and the building of bridges forbidden.

ST. PETERSBURG.

TRINITY (TROITSKY) BRIDGE

*Mid 19th century*
*Lithograph from a drawing by Jean Arnout*
*32.5 x 39.7*

*The pontoon Trinity Bridge, 500 meters long and richly decorated, was created in 1827. It connected the left bank of the Neva to the Petersburg Side. On the right bank the bridge began from Trinity Square with the Trinity Church, hence its name. It lasted for seventy years until the opening of a permanent bridge in 1903.*

NEVSKY PROSPEKT BY MOONLIGHT
*1855–59*

*Lithograph by Louis Jean Jacottet and Guillaume Louis Pierre Rêgamey from a drawing by Joseph Charlemagne*
*45 x 63*

*Nevsky Prospekt is the main street of St. Petersburg, one of its oldest thoroughfares stretching over four and a half kilometers. By the end of the 1850s, the architectural ensemble of Nevsky Prospekt had for the most part reached its final form. It was adorned by six churches of the Russian Orthodox and other faiths, the Alexandrinsky Theater, the Public Library and the City Duma (council). The bridges crossing the picturesque canals gave the Prospekt a special charm. From December to April, snow usually lay on the streets of St. Petersburg and its residents rode by sleigh along the snow-covered sidewalks. Beginning in the 1830s, Nevsky Prospekt and many other streets were lit by gas lanterns.*

THE ALEXANDRINSKY THEATER

*Mid 19th century*
*Lithograph tinted with watercolor by A. Besemann*
*38 x 50.5*

*The Imperial Alexandrinsky Drama Theater, built by the architect Carlo Rossi in the classical style, was inaugurated in 1832. The main façade of the theater faces Nevsky Prospekt and here, on the left side of the square, are two pavilions also erected by Rossi. The theater staged comedies by the famous Russian playwrights Alexander Griboyedov, Nikolai Gogol, Ivan Turgenev, and others.*

ANICHKOV BRIDGE

*Mid 19th century*
*Lithograph tinted with watercolor by Louis Jean Jacottet from a*
*drawing by Joseph Charlemagne*
*43 x 52*

This three-span bridge is located at the intersection of Nevsky
Prospekt and the Fontanka River, at the place where the city gates
stood in the 18th century. It is decorated with four bronze
compositions of horse tamers executed by Pyotr Klodt. Twice Nicholas
I gave sculptural groups, intended for the decoration of the bridge, to
European monarchs: to the Prussian king, Friedrich Wilhelm, and to
the king of Naples. In 1850, the decoration of the bridge was
completed. The building beyond the bridge with the splendid faÇades
is the palace of the Counts Beloselsky-Belozersky, erected in 1846 by
the architect Andrei Stakenschneider in the Elizabethan Baroque style
of the mid 18th century.

MODEL FOR ONE OF THE SCULPTURAL GROUPS ON THE
ANICHKOV BRIDGE

*Mid 19th century. By Pyotr Klodt*
*Cast bronze. 31 x 39 x 19*

The Anichkov Bridge across the Fontanka River on Nevsky Prospekt,
one of the oldest of St. Petersburg's bridges, was decorated in
1849–50 with four statues of horses being tamed by men.

GALLERY OF THE "PASSAGE" DEPARTMENT STORE ON
NEVSKY PROSPEKT

*1849*
*Lithograph tinted with watercolor by P. Semechkin*
*62 x 46.5*

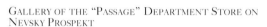

In 1848, a new type of department store appeared in St. Petersburg
where it was possible not only to make purchases but also to be
entertained. The building included a roofed, glazed gallery-
passageway between Nevsky Prospekt and Italianskaya Street, hence
the name. Stylish dresses, jewelry and other kinds of luxuries were
sold. There were also a confectioner's, cafe, restaurant and a room of
wax figures. Concerts and lectures were given in the concert hall of the
Passage.

RESTAURANT IN A HOTEL

*Mid 19th century*
*Lithograph by Victor Adam*
*39.5 x 57*

Old St.Petersburg abounded in places where people satisfied their
hunger: from fashionable restaurants to tea-rooms and snackbars
where the cheapest food was served. Every establishment had its own
reputation and its own clientele. The restaurant depicted in the
lithograph is not of a high category; it catered for the hotel's guests,
which included merchants, salesmen and petty officials.

FIGURINES OF ST. PETERSBURG STREET CHARACTERS:
RAGWOMAN, JEW WITH CLOCKS, FISHMONGER, JANITOR,
SHOEMAKER

*1820s and 1840s*
*Francis Gardner's Factory*
*Porcelain, overglaze painting*
*Height 16.5, 18, 21, 16.5, and 20.5*

These figurines were so popular that their replicas were produced,
with only slight changes, over a long period.

СТАНЦІЯ МОСКОВСКОЙ ЖЕЛѢЗНОЙ ДОРОГИ. | EMBARCADÈRE DU CHEMIN DE FER DE MOSCOU
St PETERSBOURG

ZNAMENSKAYA SQUARE

*1855–59*
*Lithograph tinted with watercolor by Louis Jean Jacottet and Aubrin*
*from a drawing by Joseph Charlemagne*
*42.5 x53*

*The square is located at the intersection of Nevsky and Ligovsky Prospekts. On the left are the chapel and portico of the Church of the Virgin of the Sign (Znamenskaya), built in 1794–1804. In 1940, the church was demolished. On the right is the Nikolaevsky Railway Station, built between 1844 and 1851 to a design by Konstantin Thon. A similar railway station was built to his design in Moscow.*

THE FIRST RAILROAD FROM ST. PETERSBURG TO PAVLOVSK

*1830s*
*Engraving by F. Martens*
*37 x 33*

*In 1837, the first railroad in Russia connected St. Petersburg with the imperial summer residences in Tsarskoye Selo and Pavlovsk.*

The Building of the Dutch Church on Nevsky
Prospekt
*1850s*
*Lithograph tinted with watercolor*
*32 x 51.5*

ANNUNCIATION (BLAGOVESHCHENSKAYA) SQUARE

*1850s*
*Lithograph by Louis Jean Jacottet and Charles Claude Bachelier*
*from a drawing by Joseph Charlemagne*
*58 x 42*

*View of Annunciation Square from the Nikolaevsky Bridge, the first*
*permanent bridge over the Neva built of cast iron. The church was*
*built for the Life-Guards Cavalry Regiment in 1844–49 to a design*
*by Konstantin Thon. It was demolished in 1929.*

THE LIFE-GUARDS CAVALRY REGIMENT PRAYING IN THE
MANÉGE IN THE PRESENCE OF EMPEROR NICHOLAS I

*1849*
*Oil on canvas*
*56 x 88*

VUE DE L'ÉGLISE PRISE A L'ANGLE DU BOULEVART DE L'AMIRAUTE

ST. ISAAC'S CATHEDRAL FROM ADMIRALTY BOULEVARD

*1845*
*Lithograph by Philippe Benois from a drawing by Auguste Montferrand*
*48.5 x 63.5*

*The first cathedral consecrated to St. Isaac of Dalmatia was built under Peter I, since the Emperor's birthday fell on the feast of St. Isaac. The cathedral was repeatedly rebuilt. Between 1818 and 1858 a new cathedral was erected to a design by Auguste Montferrand. Sculptors, artists and mosaicists worked on the cathedral's decoration. Granite for the 112 columns and the massive steps was quarried in Finland and the marble for the façades and interior in the Urals, the Baltics and Italy. St. Isaac's Cathedral is the largest religious structure in St. Petersburg.*

MONUMENT TO EMPEROR NICHOLAS I

*1858–60*
*Lithograph by Louis Jean Jacottet and Charles Claude Bachelier*
*from a drawing by Joseph Charlemagne*
*45 x 63.8*

---

*The idea of setting up the monument on St. Isaac's Square was conceived by the architect Auguste Montferrand, who also designed the pedestal. The six-meter equestrian statue was executed by Baron Pyotr Klodt. The Emperor is represented wearing the full-dress uniform of a horse-guard. The tall, massive pedestal of granite and marble is decorated with allegories of Wisdom, Power, Justice, and Faith in the form of bronze female figures with portrait features of the Emperor's wife and daughters. The monument was unveiled in 1859.*

# Alexander II

REIGNED

## 1 8 5 5 — 1 8 8 1

Grand Duke Alexander Nikolayevich, the son of Nicholas I, became Emperor of Russia at the age of thirty-seven. He was the sole, undisputed heir to the throne. Over a period of almost twenty years he had, in his position as heir, played a fairly close part in the affairs of government, occupying responsible military and state posts. Expressing his hopes for a favorable reign, the writer and democrat Alexander Herzen addressed the new Emperor from exile in London with a request to settle the two most important questions for Russia: "Sire, give freedom to the Russian word… Give land to the peasants…" Herzen was not alone in thinking this way, the whole of Russia hoped for the rapidest possible solution of the peasant question above all. And when in 1858 Alexander II declared his intention to "liberate" the serfs, Herzen's journal, *Kolokol* (The Bell), published an article dubbing the Emperor "the Liberator." From that moment the epithet "Tsar-Liberator" constantly accompanied Alexander II's name. But the "great expectations" of reform turned sour on 19 February 1861, when the statute on the liberation of the serfs was published. In its final form (after the work of commissions and committees engaged in preparing the reform), the plots of land to be allocated to the peasants were greatly reduced and amounted to only a quarter of what the serfs had had before the reform. Consequently the reform was damaging for both peasants and landowners. ■ The second major step in Alexander II's activities was the reform of the judiciary, which was a progressive move for the time, and in some of its provisions ahead of judicial legislation in the European countries. The principle of elective judges adopted in the Russian judicial statute had hitherto been applied only in the American states. ■ The new law on the press of 1865, which had been the object of such great hope and which was expected to give definite guarantees and freedom of expression, in fact turned out to be draconic and restricted the freedom of the press with new censorial requirements. ■ Despite the fact that the hoped-for freedom of the press did not come about, on the whole the period of reforms which characterized the first part of Alexander II's reign was an age when liberalism flourished in Russian legislation and so-

EMPEROR ALEXANDER II
*1861*
*By Adolf Gebens*
*Oil on canvas*
*97 x 74*

*Alexander II is shown wearing an admiral's full-dress uniform with the ribbon of the Order of St. Andrew the First-Called and the Order of St. George, 4th grade. He also wears a gold medal for the annexation of the Caucasus, two foreign decorations and medals as well as the badge for twenty-years irreproachable service. By his sword are the Orders of St. Andrew the First-Called and of St. Vladimir, 1st grade.*

cial life. One act of forgiveness and benevolence was the Emperor's decision to amnesty the Decembrists who after twenty-five years of hard labor and exile in Siberia were finally able to return. ■ The reign of Alexander II marked the beginning of the bourgeois development in the country which lasted until 1917 and the reforms he implemented promoted the emergence of capitalism. But, for the reforms to be more effective one further step was necessary – the granting of a constitution. Yet Alexander II's government proved unable to make this move. Replying to the demands of the Moscow nobility, the Emperor said: "What do you want? A constitutional form of government? […] I am prepared to put my name to any sort of constitution so long as I am certain it is of use to Russia. But I know that if I were to do that today, tomorrow Russia would fall to pieces." The constitutional issue remained unresolved and the numerous attempts made on Alexander II's life were testimony to the deepening crisis of autocracy and the intensification of the revolutionary situation. ■ In the sphere of foreign policy the Tsar's peace-loving intentions did not spare him from the necessity of having to end the Crimean War which Nicholas I had begun and sign the Treaty of Paris which was ignominious for Russia, nor from waging war against Turkey in the Balkans in 1877–78 over the liberation of Bulgaria. It also fell to Alexander II to complete, in 1864, the conquest of the Caucasus, which again his father had begun. In the Far East Russia's territory was considerably expanded through the annexation, by peaceful rather than military means, of the Amur area and the Ussuri region. As a result Russia gained an outlet to the Pacific. After the taking of the Caucasus the advance southwards continued in Central Asia, culminating in the annexation of an extensive piece of territory and the cities of Khiva, Bukhara and Tashkent. ■ During Alexander II's reign St. Petersburg gradually turned into a large capitalist city with burgeoning industry and an active business and social life, a place which attracted numerous scholars, artists and performers who found great opportunities for creative endeavor and furthered the transformation of the city itself. Noticeable changes took place in St. Petersburg's appearance. It became more complex and many-sided. For example, with the closure of the Admiralty shipyard, shipbuilding moved to a relatively small island further down the left bank of the Neva. The New Admiralty with its slipways took its place in the panorama of the Neva. In the 1870s, it was decided to remove the old maritime trade port located in the center of the city and build it closer to the sea. The construction of the Warsaw and Baltic Railway Stations in the 1850s and 1860s provided St. Petersburg with railway links to the south of Russia and the western countries. In the second half of the nineteenth century an ever-growing number of factories and works appeared in St. Petersburg, springing up on the banks of the Obvodny Canal, on the western part of Vasilyevsky Island, and in the Vyborg Side district where one of the largest was the Russian Diesel Works founded in 1862 by the industrialist Ludwig Nobel. ■ Developing industry, extensive international trade and financial activities prompted the appearance of new banks, including the Russian Private Commercial Bank for Foreign Trade opened on Bolshaya Morskaya Street in 1872. ■ Much attention was devoted to the improvement of the center of St. Petersburg. Gardens were laid out near the Admiralty and the monument to Peter the Great on Senate Square. The first water supply network with a total length of 115 kilometers came into operation. The first electric light appeared on the city's streets. In 1879, twelve electric lamps were installed on Liteiny Bridge. This same period saw the construction of the

Admiralty Embankment on the Neva, forming a single unbroken chain with the Palace and English embankments. Under Alexander II monuments were set up to Empress Catherine II (1873, sculptor Mikhail Mikeshin) and Emperor Nicholas I (1859, sculptor Pyotr Klodt). ■ After the terrorist Dmitry Karakozov made an attempt on Alexander II's life in 1866, the government undertook a series of measures aimed at the reorganization of the municipal administration. A gendarmerie was set up to carry out political surveillance of the inhabitants of St. Petersburg and the surrounding province. The Municipal Board became the executive organ of the city duma; police districts were introduced in place of the city quarters; and a city governor's office was established to exercise administrative and police control in St. Petersburg. After the introduction of the judicial reform and magistrates' courts the city was divided up into judicial districts under the magistrates. ■ All these measures, aimed at suppressing the revolutionary movement, failed to save Alexander II from a violent death. After twelve assassination attempts over the course of fifteen years, on 1 March 1881 the Emperor was fatally wounded by a bomb thrown by Ignaty Grinevitsky. ■ In 1887–1907, the Church of the Resurrection of Christ was built on the site of the fatal attack by the Catherine Canal becoming a monument to the tragically slain Emperor, whose reign had begun with such optimism and ended in catastrophe.

РУССКІЕ КРЕСТЬЯНЕ БЛАГОДАРЯТЪ ИМПЕРАТОРА АЛЕКСАНДРА II ЗА ОСВОБОЖДЕНІЕ ОТЪ КРѢПОСТНОЙ ЗАВИСИМОСТИ.
*19 Февраля 1861 г.*

Гулянье на Царицыномъ Лугу, въ С. Петербургѣ, въ день совершеннолѣтія
Его Императорскаго Высочества, Государя Наслѣдника Цесаревича и Великаго Князя
**НИКОЛАЯ АЛЕКСАНДРОВИЧА;**
8го Сентября 1859 года.

Fête on the Field of Mars

*1859*
*Lithograph from the Russkiy khudozhestvenny listok (Russian Arts*
*Leaflet),1859, No. 29*
*30.5 x 44*

*The Field of Mars was the traditional place for military reviews,*
*parades, public fêtes, and festivities in St. Petersburg.*

Peasants Thanking Alexander II for Emancipation
from Serfdom

*Mid 19th century*
*Lithograph from a drawing by B. Rozhansky*
*35.5 x 48*

*The promulgation of the Emancipation Manifesto of February 19,*
*1861, was marked by celebrations in St. Petersburg. This lithograph*
*shows one of these festive episodes on Palace Square.*

### SLEIGH RACE ON THE ICE OF THE NEVA

*1859*
*Lithograph from a drawing by Joseph Charlemagne*
*42 x 62*

*In the very center of the city, competitions between sleigh teams were held on the Neva ice before a large gathering of people.*

### VIEW OF THE ICE CASTLE IN THE "AQUARIUM" GARDEN

*1889*
*Lithograph from a drawing by Erber*
*31.5 x 41.5*

*In 1886, in the Petersburg Side district, on Kamennoostrovsky Prospekt, a fashionable amusement establishment, the Aquarium, was opened. It included a summer garden, a restaurant and a theater for operettas. An ice palace was built in the garden for the amusement of the public.*

ЛЕДЯНОЙ ЗАМОКЪ ВЪ САДУ „АКВАРIУМЪ" ВЪ СПЕТЕРБУРГЪ 1889 г.

LES MONTAGNES DE GLACE
SUR LA PLACE DE L'AMIRAUTÉ PENDANT LE CARNAVAL

**TOBOGGAN HILLS ON ADMIRALTY SQUARE DURING SHROVETIDE IN 1835**

*Mid 19th century*
*Lithograph tinted with watercolor*
*38.5 x 45.5*

*During Maslenitsa, or Shrovetide, popular fêtes were held to celebrate the end of winter. A favorite place for these gatherings from the mid 18th century was Admiralty Square, a real pleasure-ground with toboggan hills, swings and show booths.*

**A HORSE-DRAWN TRAM STUCK IN THE SNOW**

*1878*
*Drawing by G. Broling*
*25.5 x 19.2*

*In 1862, the Horse-Drawn Tram Railroads Company organized traffic with one- and two-story vehicles harnessed to a pair of horses. The speed was not great – about eight kilometers per hour. Horse-drawn trams were used mainly by clerks, workers and servants; soldiers were allowed to travel only on the open platforms. From 1907, the electric tram gradually superseded the horse-drawn tram.*

VIEW OF THE RUSSIAN-AMERICAN RUBBER MANUFACTORY
IN ST. PETERSBURG. 1892

*Chromolithograph*
*65 x 77.5*

---

*In 1860, the Russian-American Rubber Manufactory was founded in*
*St. Petersburg, maintaining a complete monopoly on rubber*
*production in Russia until the end of the 19th century. In 1908, the*
*firm was renamed Triangle and during the Soviet period, Red*
*Triangle*

BADGE OF THE MAYOR OF ST. PETERSBURG

*1870*
*Silver-plated white metal*
*8.9 x 6.4*

CHAIN WITH THE BADGE OF A MEMBER OF THE ST. PETERSBURG MUNICIPAL EXECUTIVE BOARD

*1870*
*Silver-plated brass and white metal*
*9.3 x 6.6, length of chain 106*

CHAIN WITH THE BADGE OF A JUDGE, INSCRIBED LAW ON EIGHT COLUMNS UNDER THE CROWN

*1870*
*Patinated and gilt bronze*
*9.6 x 8.1, length of chain 115*

ATTEMPT ON THE LIFE OF ALEXANDER II, MARCH 1, 1881

*1881*
*Lithograph by D. Rudnev*
*46.5 x 51.5*

*On March 1, 1881, after many unsuccessful attempts, revolutionary terrorists belonging to the "Will of the People" organization fatally wounded Alexander II as he rode in his carriage along the embankment of the Catherine Canal. Ignaty Grinevitsky, a former student of the Technological Institute, threw the bomb at the Tsar. Later, on this spot the Church of the Resurrection of Christ, commonly known as Our Savior on the Spilled Blood, was built.*

ПОКУШЕНІЕ НА ЖИЗНЬ ЕГО ИМПЕРАТОРСКАГО ВЕЛИЧЕСТВА ГОСУДАРЯ ИМПЕРАТОРА АЛЕКСАНДРА II—ВЗРЫВЪ ВТОРАГО СНАРЯДА, 1го МАРТА.

Alexander III.

# Alexander III

REIGNED

## 1 8 8 1   1 8 9 4

By the time he came to the throne the heir was a completely mature man, with a fully formed character, fixed habits, views and patterns of behavior. ■ Although he ascended the throne under exceptional circumstances – as the result of the tragic killing of his father – Alexander III gave no signs of confusion. ■ Autocracy, Orthodoxy and Nationality *(narodnost)* – the triple slogan constantly appealed to under Nicholas I became in essence the foundation of Alexander III's reign. In truth, however, it was already no longer possible to bring back the "good old days," and the slogan became nothing more than a rhetorical device. Nevertheless a reactionary course had been proclaimed. Alexander glossed over his turn to the right with a whole parcel of measures to strengthen the ailing welfare of the peasantry. From 1882 onwards, the Peasant Bank began to function busily in St. Petersburg; a law restricted the working hours of minors in factories; a factory inspectorate was established; and the capitation tax was abolished for the entire population. ■ The new sovereign chose the suburban palace at Gatchina, not far from St. Petersburg, as his chief residence. When in St. Petersburg he usually followed his earlier custom of staying at the Anichkov Palace. The "prisoner of Gatchina," as the Tsar came to be jokingly known, did not withdraw into family life and day-to-day work. Alexander frequently traveled to the capital returning the same day. Everything went on much as before: state receptions in the Winter Palace, balls, regimental festivities, weddings, the unveiling of monuments, funerals and, in a tradition established from 1884 onwards, the gifts to the Emperor of two new Easter eggs each year from the court jeweler Pierre Faberge. ■ At the same time the Emperor

PORTRAIT OF EMPEROR
ALEXANDER III

*1880s*
*Engraving by A. Heger*
*26.8 x 18*

made a firm decision to put an end to the growth of criminality in the capital and to give its citizens complete peace of mind. To punish his personal enemies, as he regarded his father's murderers, he erected an enormous complex for the solitary confinement of all potential revolutionaries infected with liberalism, nihilism or socialism. This edifice went down in St. Petersburg history as the *Kresty* (Crosses) and political prisoners were among its first occupants. ■ Despite the threat of terrorist bombs, obtrusive security, sometimes exceeding all the bounds of common sense, irritated Alexander III. Disregarding, or braving the danger, the Tsar continued to ride about in a carriage fitted with bells like a French mail-coach so that it could be heard at great distances. ■ Having declared himself a truly Russian Orthodox sovereign, Alexander strove by all means possible to make himself typically Russian: a spade beard, a round lambskin hat and wide trousers tucked into boots. St. Petersburg, too, changed its attire: the police wore short Russian caftans with a slanting collar and lambskin caps; the gendarmes were given caps with a red crown and white plumes as if to make sure they could be seen from a distance. High boots were introduced in the army and the cavalry wore wide blue-gray trousers. Everybody accepted the new uniforms considering them perhaps less attractive, but more practical and inexpensive. ■ In this period St. Petersburg was adorned with monuments to Russian cultural figures, scholars and statesmen: the first memorials in Russia to the country's great poet Alexander Pushkin was unveiled, while others immortalized included the poet Vasily Zhukovsky, the scholar Mikhail Lomonosov, the scholar and explorer of Asia Nikolai Przevalski and three Russian eighteenth-century statesmen who died in the struggle against German domination – Artemy Volynsky, Pyotr Eropkin and Alexander Khrushchov. ■ It is a generally known fact that Alexander III disliked non-Russians: Finns, Poles, Armenians, Jews. The spirit of militant nationalism led to the organization of various forms of constraints and persecutions of the non-Russian and non-Orthodox, and also of different sects. Nevertheless, during his reign the city's synagogue was built and opened (1883–93), the uncensored Jewish-Russian journal *Voskhod* (Dawn) was founded and the banking houses of Wawelberg and Ginzburg flourished. The baptised Jew Anton Rubinstein was director of the St. Petersburg Conservatoire and the opera he wrote, *The Merchant Kalashnikov*, was one of Alexander III's favorites. The first biographical article about Alexander III appeared in the encyclopedia produced in 1890 by Ilya Efron, the son of a businessman and Talmudic scholar. General Nikolai Rosenbach felt at ease in the Emperor's retinue; Finns continued to serve in the security force at the palace. The Finnish Light Steam Navigation Company, reorganized by Major Rafail von Hartmann, expanded its activities to embrace all the internal water routes in St. Petersburg. ■ The concern about the fortunes of the country in trade and industry, which had begun to be shown immediately after Alexander III's accession, grew stronger with every year. At this time St. Petersburg became the largest financial center in the country. Its banking houses acted as founders of almost all the banks in Russia. ■ Throughout his entire reign Alexander III never took the country to war, and more than that, he managed to convince the entire world in the genuiness of his desire for peace, so that everywhere the Emperor was honorably known as the Peacemaker. ■ Alexander III's reign was marked by the implementation of a large complex of works positively affecting the development and improvement of the city. In the mid 1880s, public gardens were laid out on Pokrovskaya Square off Grechesky Prospekt, as was a boulevard on the Obvodny Canal, while another boulevard was begun on the site of the Ligovka Canal which had been piped underground. ■ In 1884, the stretch of Nevsky Prospekt between the Moika and Fontanka Rivers was given electric street lighting, and five years later filtered water flowed from the city's taps for the first time. The city duma was given control of the four largest municipal hospitals. The first telephone station was opened. Numerous public buildings added to the variety of St. Petersburg architecture: the Civil Engineering Institute, the building of the State Council archive, a municipal building housing various civil institutions, and a whole range of structures for the rapidly developing industry in the city. In 1887, at the Emperor's suggestion the planning of the Grand-Ducal Burial Vault was begun. ■ Fifteen years after his death, on the square in front of the Nikolayevsky Railway Station, an equestrian statue designed by the talented Russian sculptor Paulo Trubetskoi was set up – St. Petersburg's monument to Alexander III.

DESIGN FOR THE DECORATION OF THE KNIGHTS' HALL IN
THE ANICHKOV PALACE

*1874*
*Draft by Hippolyte Monighetti*
*Watercolor and pencil*
*63.5 x 95*

*From the middle of the 1860s, the Anichkov Palace on Nevsky
Prospekt belonged to Grand Duke Alexander Alexandrovich (the
future Emperor Alexander III). The architect Monighetti
reconstructed the palace for the Grand Duke in 1874. One of the halls
was decorated with large painted panels depicting scenes from
knightly life in the Middle Ages.*

TRIPTYCH WITH PORTRAITS OF EMPEROR ALEXANDER III,
HIS WIFE MARIA FEDOROVNA AND THE HEIR NIKOLAI
ALEXANDROVICH (THE FUTURE EMPEROR NICHOLAS II)

*1886*
*Three photographs, two of which are tinted by hand; wood, gilding*
*75 x 56*

NEVSKY PROSPEKT BY THE ANICHKOV BRIDGE

*1886*
*By Alexander Beggrow*
*Oil on canvas*
*60.5 x 89.5*

*View toward the Admiralty the tower of which concludes the vista of Nevsky Prospekt. Left, in the foreground, is the palace built in 1847–48 by Andrei Stakenschneider for the Princes Beloselsky-Belozersky. In 1884, Grand Duke Sergei Alexandrovich, the brother of Alexander III, became the new owner of the palace. Charity soirées were held in the concert hall, where famous musicians including Tchaikovsky and Rubinstein performed. The four-story house on the right (No. 68) is of interest as it was the residence of several well-known writers such as Ivan Turgenev, Vissarion Belinsky, and others.*

HOCK-CUP SET: EGG-SHAPED VESSEL AND SIX WINEGLASSES

*1880s–90s*

*The service was made at the Petersburg Glass Factory, founded in 1704 and in 1890 merged with the Imperial Porcelain Factory. Now it is an independent enterprise again, known as the Decorative Glassware Factory.*
*Matt glass, painted in gold and enamels*
*Height 30.5 and 7.2*

MENU OF THE ELDERS' DINNER ON THE OCCASION OF
ALEXANDER III'S CORONATION. MAY 21, 1883

*Chromolithograph by Nikolai Karazin*
*33.7 x 23'*
*List of dishes at the royal table:*
*Main course – French pullet and pheasant*
*Salad and fresh cucumber*
*Truffle in champagne*
*Sweet dishes: peaches Imperial, ice cream, dessert*

*During the coronation festivities, dinners were given for*
*representatives of the various estates of Russia in the presence of the*
*royal couple. The elders (starshiny) presented gifts to the Emperor*
*from the various nationalities inhabiting Russia.*

STEEL KNOT, TIED WHEN COLD

*1892*
*St. Petersburg Putilov Metal Works*
*Engraved steel, contained in a case of leather and silk*
*9 x 22*

*In the late 19th century the welded spikes of Putilov steel for
railroads were renowned for their quality. This knot was displayed
at an exhibition of architects in 1892*

COMMERCIAL POSTER. GALOSHES FROM THE TRIANGLE
FIRM. ST. PETERSBURG.
*After 1908*
*Chromolithograph*
*49.5 x 35*

# Nicholas II

REIGNED

*1 8 9 4*    *1 9 1 7*

In the ruling Romanov dynasty Nicholas II was one of the youngest Russian tsars. He ascended the throne and married almost at the same time, having to assume two high duties at once. Addressing the members of the State Council in the Anichkov Palace, the new Emperor declared: "May God help me to bear the burden of serving the State that has been imposed on me prematurely." And that burden was not long in making itself felt. The coronation festivities that started so well in the spring of 1896 culminated in a real national tragedy after a mere three days. Due to incredible chaos and lack of organization, the distribution of royal gifts to the public on Khodynka Field in Moscow ended in enormous loss of life. As Pierre Gilliard, the former tutor of Tsarevich Alexis, later noted in his memoirs, "with this event fate seemed to have started its hunt for the royal couple." The tragedy on Khodynka Field, as well as the shooting down of a peaceful procession on Palace Square in January 9, 1905 which marked the beginning of the first Russian revolution, were incidents that must have haunted the Emperor for the rest of his life. ■ Subsequent events connected with the fall of the imperial House of Romanov decided the fates of hundreds of thousands of people. Of all the contributions to this historic drama made by "members of the aristocracy, the bearers of court ranks… bankers, publishers, lawyers, professors and other public figures on whom the Empire lavished its generosities," the imperial family's was by no means the least. ■ In this context Gilliard's idea that it was not the monarchy which was overthrown by a "billow risen from the depths" but, on the contrary, it was the monarchy's "disaster which raised such a formidable wave that swept over all of Russia," does not seem so casuistic. ■ The holy of holiest of Russian autocracy – the imperial power – became affected by the eroding skepticism of the time and was finally stripped of its sacred shroud. Behind all kinds of individual stories, conveying the flavor of everyday life in the "holy" state, lies one common theme – its moral and physical exhaustion. This can be easily gleaned from such seemingly insignificant things as the private life of the royal family, the falling prestige and solemnity of palace ceremonies, the morganatic marriages contracted by the ruling family and,

EMPEROR NICHOLAS II

*1910s*
*By Ernst Liphart*
*Oil on canvas*
*91 x 77*

*The Emperor is shown wearing a frock-coat of the special company of the Marines who crewed the royal vessel with a captain's shoulder strap, the Order of St. Vladimir of the 4th grade and the badge of the Marines.*

last but not least, the presence in intimate court circles of strange people which could not but discredit the royal dynasty. The destruction of the Emperor's crystal palace is demonstrated by the appearance of all kinds of mysterious apostles of mysticism: from 1900 on, the court was visited by Monsieur Philippe, the Austrian Schenk, another Frenchman Papuce as well as home-grown enchanters – the pilgrim Darya Osipovna, the fortuneteller "Barefoot" Matrena, the holy fool Mit'ka Kozelsky, Antony the Wanderer, and so on. Psychological instability at court manifested itself in a passion for spiritualism. All these people cared neither for the grandeur of supreme power, nor for Russia herself. As Mikhail Rodzianko, Chairman of the State Duma, wrote, "no revolutionary propaganda could have done what the presence of these people did." In the reign of Nicholas II etiquette was much less strictly observed than in the times of Alexander III. Thus, for example, when the imperial family visited the theater, all the relatives used to gather during the intervals in the royal foyer without any special invitation. Grand dukes behaved in a more than democratic manner, taking the liberty of sitting when the tsar was standing; they smoked heavily to the displeasure of the grand duchesses who made futile attempts to dispel the smoke with their fans and kerchiefs. The notion that the private life of the royal family should be a model for its subjects had been completely lost. The sanctions that had been imposed on the protagonists of morganatic marriages, sometimes extremely severe, uneven and unjustified, were repealed in a short while. The guilty were pardoned and returned to Russia, regaining their former position. But wounded pride made itself felt and former relations were not restored. The decline of the monarchic principle was quite obvious in this sphere. ■ Even the grand Petersburgian balls in the Winter Palace were a thing of the past: the last such ball took place on January 19, 1904. Nicholas's daughters were not destined to take part in one of these balls. In 1914, when the war broke out, Olga Nikolayevna was almost nineteen while Tatyana Nikolayevna just turned sixteen. They were lucky enough to attend two or three evening parties arranged by their aunt, Grand Duchess Olga Alexandrovna. ■ Yet outwardly all was fine in St. Petersburg. Everything proclaimed that it was the capital of the Russian emperors: royal carriages with servants in decorative liveries, pink pearls and diamonds glistening in the showcases of numerous jewelry shops. It seemed that a certain decline of fashionable life, especially noticeable after the revolutionary events of 1904–05, was now abating, that from the 1910s high society was returning to its former ways and customs. Men went to horseraces, drank and played cards. Bands played in the parks and gardens, and steamships carried the merrymaking public to the islands. Every day the auditorium of the Mariinsky Theater was filled to capacity. The city celebrated the Bicentenary of St. Petersburg, Tsarskoye Selo, the Monastery of the Holy Trinity, Russia's victories in the Great Northern War, the Centenary of the Borodino Battle, the Tercentenary of the House of Romanov, and so on and so on. In the number of commemorative medals issued, Nicholas II excelled all his predecessors. Beginning in 1902, such awards flowed as if from a horn of plenty. ■ The Emperor wanted to win the hearts of his subjects not through palace ceremonies but through the revival of popular festivities. Arranging a grand masked ball in January 1903, Nicholas above all aspired to "return, at least for a night, to the glorious past of his family." From the fall of 1904 the idea was repeatedly expressed to call the State Duma (a body with consultative powers) by the traditional Russian title of "Zemsky Sobor." The extraordinarily pompous ceremonial that marked its opening was planned by the imperial couple; both the Empress and the Dowager wore white sarafans and pearl-studded *kokoshniki*-headdresses, and maids of honor were also dressed in Russian costumes. This was in fact an attempt to shield the monarchy from an approaching storm, to reaffirm its prestige at the most difficult period of its existence on the threshold of a tragic finale. On the other hand, however, this brings to mind a humorous but sad anecdote about Paul I who allegedly asked his murderers to delay his assassination a little as he had not managed to work out the ceremonial for his own burial. ■ As a matter of fact, the Emperor's presence in St. Petersburg was an extremely irregular occurrence. It might be said that there was no emperor in St. Petersburg. Having left the city, Nicholas locked himself and his family away in Tsarskoye Selo. But even abandoned by the Emperor, St. Petersburg remained the capital of the Russian Empire, the center of officialdom and bureaucracy. The early twentieth century was marked by a rapid increase in the number of officials which by 1913 reached 70,000. The Petersburg garrison that mainly consisted of Life-Guards regiments (the Finnish, Semyonovsky, Horse-Guards etc.) numbered almost 48,000 servicemen; there was one soldier for every 39 inhabitants. The nobility comprised 7.5% of the entire population, or 138,000, and by 1913 the city had a population of 2,126,600. ■ The reign of Nicholas II is associated with a brilliant upsurge in Russian culture, art and science, a period known as the "silver age" in culture and the arts. St. Petersburg was the home of such outstanding poets and writers as Alexander Blok, Nikolai Gumilev, Anna Akhmatova, Andrei Bely, Dmitry Merezhkovsky, Vyacheslav Ivanov, Zinaida Gippius and Fedor Sologub, the philosophers Nikolay Berdyaev and Vasily Rozanov, to name but two, and the physiologist Ivan Pavlov who won a Nobel Prize in 1909. ■ Around 1913, St. Petersburg became the center of the Futurist movement in Russia. In that year, the first Futurist opera, *Victory over the Sun*, was staged in the city, with the sets contributed by Kasimir Malevich, the founder of Suprematism in painting, the text written by Alexei Kruchenykh and Velimir Khlebnikov, and the music composed by Mikhail Matiushin. ■ With the start of the First World War, the abdication of Nicholas II from the throne and the revolution of 1917, this tempestuous development came to a halt. ■ When he was away from St. Petersburg, Nicholas never yearned for it. Neither St. Petersburg, nor its regal heart, the Winter Palace, held any attraction for him. The abdication from the throne was at the same time an abdication from St. Petersburg. Having rejected it for ever, Nicholas dreamed of returning to Russia after the end of the war. After a long stay abroad, he wanted to settle down privately with his family somewhere in the Crimea for the rest of his life. He would never have pronounced the phrase which his dying grandfather Alexander II uttered on the site of the assassination attempt: "To the palace... and there to die."

THE ROYAL COUPLE ATTENDING A BALL IN THE WINTER
PALACE

*1896*
*Drawing by K. Brozh*
*49 x 69*

*A ball at the Winter Palace in the presence of Emperor Nicholas II*
*and his wife, Empress Alexandra Fedorovna.*

MENU OF THE SUPPER ON THE OCCASION OF THE
CORONATION OF NICHOLAS II, MAY 20, 1896
*Chromolithograph*
*37.5 x 25*
*List of dishes:*
*Strong grouse soup*
*Assorted pies*
*Sterlet Italian*
*Fried fattened fowl and game*
*Swiss salad*
*Ice cream with raspberry sauce*

*One of the most brilliant receptions on the occasion of the coronation*
*of Nicholas II was given by the Emperor's uncle Grand Duke Sergei*
*Alexandrovich. The menu illustration was contributed by the famous*
*artist Viktor Vasnetsov. The coronation scene is stylized in the*
*manner of ancient Russian chronicle miniatures. The Emperor and*
*Empress are shown in Old Russian princely attire.*

MENU OF THE COURT EASTER TABLE AND BREAKFAST.
1903 BY C. YAGUZHINSKY

*Chromolithograph*
*31.4 x 18.2*
*The Easter table:*
*Paskha, eggs*
*Sturgeon, beluga, salmon, pike-perch, stellate sturgeon, pheasant,*
*partridge, black grouse*
*Hazel-hens, ducks, lamb, ham, tongue*
*Beef on the bone, Yaroslavl veal*
*Breakfast:*
*Turtle soup, partridge and quail pies, burbot with liver*
*Chicken with truffles*
*Salad, mousse.*

---

*In Russia, many customs and popular beliefs were connected with*
*Easter and the Easter table.*
*For the Easter table, paskha (a sweet dish made of curds and eggs),*
*and kulich (a cake of cylindrical form made from fancy pastry) were*
*prepared. The main element of the Easter table was the colored eggs.*
*Eggs were colored with factory-made powders as well as by old folk*
*methods – onion skins (to produce orange and brown colors) and silk*
*cloth (for a marble effect in the staining).*
*For the court Easter table, eggs were also painted in watercolors*
*after drawings by famous artists who contributed drawings for the*
*menu as well.*
*The Easter meal began at dawn, immediately after people returned*
*from church. After forty days of fasting, the Easter table had a*
*staggering abundance of meat dishes.*

### EASTER EGG WITH THE MONOGRAM OF NICHOLAS II

*1894–1900s*
*Imperial Porcelain Factory*
*Porcelain, colored glaze, polished and matt gilding*
*Height 10.5*

*The production of monogrammed Easter eggs started under*
*Alexander III and was always strictly limited, varying from 50 to*
*100, or to 150 pieces in the 1910s. They appeared in large numbers*
*during the First World War, as eggs of small and medium size were*
*presented to the rank and file at the front and field hospitals.*

### EASTER EGG

*1890s–1900s*
*Imperial Porcelain Factory*
*Height 9.3*

*Porcelain, colored glaze*
*At Easter it is customary for Christians to present each other with*
*painted eggs. Easter eggs covered with colored glaze were produced by*
*the Imperial Porcelain Factory from 1892 to the 1910s.*
*The so-called "ordinary" eggs were the most numerous and painted*
*with flowers and ornamental designs. Eggs bearing images of saints*
*and scenes of the twelve principal Christian feasts comprised the*
*highest category.*

### EASTER EGG WITH THE IMAGE OF THE APOSTLE PAUL

*Second half, 19th century*
*Imperial Porcelain Factory*
*Porcelain, overglaze painting, polished and matt gilding*
*Height 11.3*

### EASTER EGG WITH THE IMAGE OF SAINTLY PRINCESS OLGA, THE FIRST CHRISTIAN IN RUS

*1900s*
*Imperial Porcelain Factory*
*Porcelain, overglaze painting*
*Height 11.3*

*Based on the fresco by Viktor Nesterov in the Cathedral of St.*
*Vladimir in Kiev.*

MODEL FOR THE STATUE OF PETER I

*Late 19th century. By Alexander Opekushin*
*Chased patinated bronze. 41 x 27 x 58*

*Made for the Bicentenary of St. Petersburg (1903) as a model for the monument to the founder of the city.*
*Until the early 1950s it stood on the railing of Peter I's tomb in the Peter and Paul Cathedral.*

JUBILEE WINEGLASS MADE FOR THE BICENTENARY OF ST. PETERSBURG

*1903*
*Dulev Factory of the Matvei Kuznetsov Company*
*Porcelain, printing*
*Height 9*

*In the late 19th and early 20th centuries the porcelain and faience industry was dominated by the Matvei Kuznetsov Company, which incorporated eight large factories, including that of Francis Gardner. The company produced about half of all Russian ceramics. Its articles reflected current trends in art, such as the Art Nouveau style with its interest to natural forms, neo-Russian tendencies, and also the traditions of Russian hand-painted decoration.*

SOUVENIR KERCHIEFS WITH 26 VIEWS OF ST. PETERSBURG COMMEMORATING THE BICENTENARY OF THE CITY.

*1903*
*Silk, print. 39 x 42*

MENU OF THE CELEBRATION DINNER AND CONCERT
PROGRAM ON THE OCCASION OF THE 300TH ANNIVERSARY
OF THE HOUSE OF ROMANOV. 1913. BY IVAN BILIBIN

*Chromolithograph*
*43 x 16.3*
*List of dishes: Turtle soup, fowl soup, pies.*
*Dvina sterlet in champagne*
*Moscow fillet of veal*
*Duck in aspic*
*Apple sauce*
*Punch Victoria.*

*In 1913, celebrations marking the 300th Anniversary of the House of
Romanov took place in all the cities of Russia. The event was
observed with particular pomp in St. Petersburg and Moscow.
Festive church services were held, monuments laid and exhibitions
opened. In St. Petersburg, dinners were given at which
commemorative medals and goblets were presented. The decoration of
the festivities was carried out in the Old Russian style.*

SOUVENIR GOBLETS, WINEGLASSES, KERCHIEFS ETC.,
PRESENTED AT DIFFERENT CELEBRATIONS IN THE REIGN
OF NICHOLAS II

*1. Goblet with a portrait of Peter I. For the bicentenary of the victory
over the Swedes at Lesnaya*
*1908*
*Tin, colored print. Height 12*

*2. Goblet commemorating the centenary of the Izhora Works*
*1903*
*Tin, colored print. Height 17*

*3. Pencil-box commemorating the Tercentenary of the Romanov
Dynasty*
*1913*
*Tin, colored print. Height*

*4. Goblet with a lid for the Bicentenary of St. Petersburg*
*1903*

*Tin, colored print. Height 20*

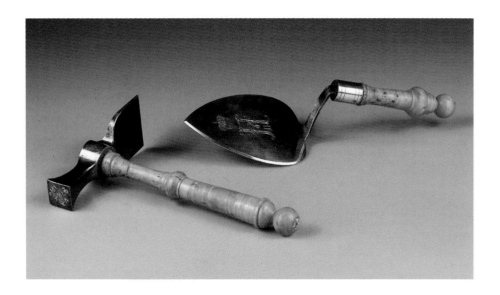

HAMMER AND TROWEL WITH THE MONOGRAMS OF
NICHOLAS II AND ALEXANDRA FEDOROVNA

*1910s*
*These articles were intended for the founding ceremony of government*
*or public office buildings in the presence of Their Imperial Majesties.*
*Metal, Karelian birch. 22.5 x 7.5; 18.5 x 4.5*

FOUNDATION STONES WITH MONOGRAMS OF NICHOLAS II
AND EMPRESS ALEXANDRA FEDOROVNA
*1914*
*These stones were intended for the founding ceremony of the building*
*of the Life-Guards Cavalry Regiment in the presence of Nicholas II.*
*Foundation stone of jasper: 21.7 x 9.8 x 6.3*
*Foundation stone of granite: 20.3 x 10.3 x 5.2*

THE NEVA BY VASILYEVSKY ISLAND

*1911*
*By Alexander Beggrow*
*Oil on plywood*
*41.5 x 60.5*

*During the 18th and early 19th centuries, the Neva and its channels
served as the main transport arteries of St. Petersburg. A significant
proportion of loads were delivered by water: provisions, building
materials etc. Foreign goods were imported and Russian-made
products exported.*
*Even after the opening, in 1885, of the Sea Canal and the transfer of
the Seaport to Gutuev Island, wharfs in the city center continued to
function for a long time and there was a constant traffic of sea and
river vessels, loaded barges, tugs, and boats on the Neva.*
*Seen in the distance is the embankment of the Neva's left bank with
the buildings of the Winter Palace, the Admiralty and the Senate.*

VASE WITH A RIVERSCAPE

*1903*
*Imperial Factory*
*Many-layered glass, deep etching, engraving. The bottom is engraved*
*with the monogram of Nicholas II: N II*
*Height 18*

At the turn of the twentieth century the technique invented by the
French artist Emile Gallé became very popular. Many-layered
colored semi-translucent glass, produced by this imperial factory, was
etched with hydrofluoric acid and decorated with a characteristic Art-
Nouveau pattern in relief against a smoky or other light-colored
background. Apart from etching the surface to a different depth, the
vases were also carved.

SCULPTURE: LADY WITH A MASK

*1910. After a model of 1906 by Konstantin Somov*
*Imperial Porcelain Factory*
*Porcelain, overglaze painting*
*Height 22.4*

In the late 19th and early 20th centuries the Imperial Porcelain
Factory turned out a large number of articles in the Art Nouveau
style, making good use of stylized and retrospective forms. Porcelain
articles were painted after cartoons by famous artists such as Ivan
Bilibin, Evgeny Lanceray, Sergei Chekhonin, Konstantin Simonov,
and Sergei Sudeikin.

SCULPTURAL GROUP: THE RAPE OF EUROPE

*1920s. After a model of 1915 by Valentin Serov*
*Porcelain; height 23.6*

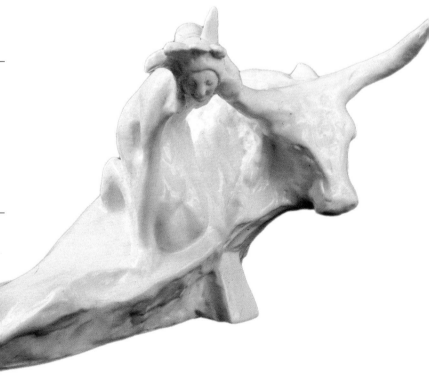

DISH WITH SCENES FROM THE RUSSIAN FOLK EPIC SADKO

*1920s*
*Manufactured at the "Gorn" (Forge) Factory (formerly the*
*Geldwein-Vaulin Ceramics workshops at Kikerino, near St.*
*Petersburg) from the original dish of 1899–1900 by the painter*
*Mikhail Vrubel*
*Majolica, colored glaze*
*47 x 58*

*In the late 19th and early 20th centuries the leading artistic centers*
*were the Imperial Porcelain Factory and some minor pottery*
*workshops, sponsored by rich patrons of art. The art of majolica was*
*revived at the factory in Kikerino. Many of its articles were decorated*
*with polychrome lustrous glaze of iridescent hues. The technique was*
*worked out by the talented ceramist Pyotr Vaulin. Fine examples of*
*majolica were produced by the painter Mikhail Vrubel whose*
*experiments in ceramics drew particular attention.*

**ВОЕННЫЙ 5¹⁰/₂₀ ЗАЕМЪ.**
**ЦѢЛЬ ЗАЙМА–УСКОРИТЬ ПОБѢДУ**
**НАДЪ ВРАГОМЪ.**

PATRIOTIC POSTER FROM THE FIRST WORLD WAR.
1915–16

*Chromolithograph*
*67 x 100*

*The introduction of the Russian coat of arms in the poster sheet was
to underline the importance of everyone's participation in the war
loan scheme.. The 5.5% loan was issued in Russia in 1915–16.
The First World War stimulated a rise of patriotic sentiment among
St. Petersburg's artists. Outstanding performers gave concerts to help
war victims and theaters produced plays dedicated to the Russian
army. Patriotic military posters were printed in mass editions.*

SOUVENIR KERCHIEFS ON THE THEME OF THE TRIPLE
ALLIANCE AND THE ENTENTE

*Early 20th century*
*Cotton fabric (calico), printed graphics. 62 x 59*

*Humorous pictures of European countries with commentaries
Such souvenirs were produced in large numbers. They were presented
at different celebrations, meetings and gala dinners. Apart from
souvenirs, the participants of gala dinners were given one or two
bottles of wine, dishes from the festive table (fried chicken, pieces of
ham, quail and the like) and different sweetmeats and candy.*

SPOUT CUP FOR THE WOUNDED IN THE FIRST WORLD WAR.
1914

*1910s*
*Matvei Kuznetsov Company (?)*
*Porcelain, painting, gilding*
*Height 7.4*

POSTERS BY THE PUBLISHING HOUSE TODAY'S LUBOK.

*Designed by Kasimir Malevich, captions by Vladimir Mayakovsky.*
*1914*

*Kaiser Wilhelm*

*Lithograph*
*55.5 x 36.9*

*Wilhelm Carousel*

*Lithograph*
*37.3 x 57.9*

The very first shots of the First World War in 1914 were echoed in
the popular print, the lubok. Hundreds of thousands of brightly
colored pictures flew off to the various ends of Russia, outstripping
newspapers and government reports. The lubok carried a blind faith
in victory, not tolerating thoughts of failure.
At the publishing house Today's Lubok, popular prints were
produced by the famous artists Aristarkh Lentulov, David Burliuk
and Kasimir Malevich, while Vladimir Mayakovsky wrote verses for
the pictures

"BLOODY SUNDAY", JANUARY 9, 1905 ON PALACE SQUARE.

*Early 20th centyry*
*Lithograph. 59,0x102,0*

*While headed towards the Winter Palace with a petition of their needs, a peaceful procession of Petersburg workers was fired on by government forces. The events of January 9 were the beginning of the first revolution.*

# I

# Актъ

объ отреченіи Государя Императора НИКОЛАЯ II отъ Престола Государства Россійскаго въ пользу Великаго Князя МИХАИЛА АЛЕКСАНДРОВИЧА.

### СТАВКА. НАЧАЛЬНИКУ ШТАБА.

Въ дни великой борьбы съ внѣшнимъ врагомъ, стремящимся почти три года поработить нашу родину, Господу Богу угодно было ниспослать Россіи новое тяжкое испытаніе. Начавшіяся внутреннія народныя волненія грозятъ бѣдственно отразиться на дальнѣйшемъ веденіи упорной войны. Судьба Россіи, честь геройской нашей арміи, благо народа, все будущее дорогого нашего Отечества требуютъ доведенія войны во что бы то ни стало до побѣднаго конца. Жестокій врагъ напрягаетъ послѣднія силы и уже близокъ часъ, когда доблестная армія наша, совмѣстно со славными нашими союзниками, сможетъ окончательно сломить врага. Въ эти рѣшительные дни въ жизни Россіи почли Мы долгомъ совѣсти облегчить народу нашему тѣсное единеніе и сплоченіе всѣхъ силъ народныхъ для скорѣйшаго достиженія побѣды и, въ согласіи съ Государственною Думою, признали Мы за благо отречься отъ Престола Государства Россійскаго и сложить съ Себя Верховную власть. Не желая разстаться съ любимымъ сыномъ Нашимъ, Мы передаемъ наслѣдіе Наше Брату Нашему Великому Князю Михаилу Александровичу и благословляемъ Его на вступленіе на Престолъ Государства Россійскаго. Заповѣдуемъ Брату Нашему править дѣлами государственными въ полномъ и ненарушимомъ единеніи съ представителями народа въ законодательныхъ учрежденіяхъ на тѣхъ началахъ, кои будутъ ими установлены, принеся въ томъ ненарушимую присягу. Во имя горячо любимой родины призываемъ всѣхъ вѣрныхъ сыновъ Отечества къ исполненію своего святого долга передъ Нимъ, повиновеніемъ Царю въ тяжелую минуту всенародныхъ испытаній и помочь Ему, вмѣстѣ съ представителями народа, вывести Государство Россійское на путь побѣды, благоденствія и славы. Да поможетъ Господь Богъ Россіи.

г. Псковъ. 2 марта 15 час. 3 мин. 1917 года.

НИКОЛАЙ.

Министръ Императорскаго Двора генералъ-адъютантъ
графъ Фредериксъ.

---

THE ANNOUNCEMENT OF THE ABDICATION OF EMPEROR

*Nicholas II. March 2, 1917*
*Paper, printed text*
*35.5 x 27.8*

---

# Ac t

## ON THE ABDICATION OF HIS MAJESTY THE EMPEROR NICHOLAS II FROM THE THRONE OF THE RUSSIAN STATE IN FAVOR OF GRAND DUKE MIKHAIL ALEXANDROVICH

### STAVKA. TO THE CHIEF OF STAFF

In the days of the great struggle against an external enemy who has been striving for almost three years to enslave our Homeland, the Lord has been pleased to impose on Russia a new terrible trial. The popular domestic disturbances that have begun threaten to have a calamitous effect on the further conduct of the stubborn war. The fate of Russia, the honor of our heroic army, the well-being of the people, all the future of our dear Homeland, demand that the war be prosecuted to its victorious end, cost that what it may. The savage enemy is straining his last strength, and the hour is already close when our valorous army together with our glorious allies will be able to break the enemy once and for all. In these decisive days in the life of Russia, we have considered it a duty of conscience to ease our people's establishment of close unity and the consolidation of all the nation's forces to achieve victory in the shortest time and, in agreement with the State Duma, we have acknowledged that it will be of benefit to abdicate from the Throne of the Russian State and to lay aside the supreme power. Not wishing to be parted from our beloved son, we transfer our

*Appendix*

*Biographies of the Emperors*

# PETER I.
## 1672–1725

The third son of Tsar Alexei Mikhailovich, and the only son by his second wife Natalia Kirillovna Naryshkina. Born on May 30, 1672, in Moscow. His father's death in 1676 unleashed the violent antagonism between the two aristocratic clans of the Miloslavsky and the Naryshkin families, and shattered the calm and security of his childhood. In April 1682, after the death of Tsar Fedor Alexeyevich, ten-year-old Peter was elected and proclaimed tsar, but in May the joint reign of the two remaining male heirs, Peter and Ivan, was established. As the new tsars were still children, their elder sister Sophia was proclaimed regent. In fact, until 1689 Peter and his mother lived at Preobrazhenskoye, near Moscow, avoiding the Kremlin and only appearing in the capital on formal occasions. In 1689, Peter married Eudoxia Lopukhina, the daughter of a minor noble, who in 1690 gave him a son, Tsarevich Alexei.

From 1689 Peter and his supporters exercised virtually complete control in the country. In 1699, he forced his wife Eudoxia and his sisters Sophia and Marfa to take the veil. In 1718, charged with plotting against Peter, Tsarevich Alexei was condemned to death and executed. He was buried in the Peter and Paul Cathedral.

In 1712, Peter I formalized and publicly proclaimed his marriage to Ekaterina Alexeyevna (née Martha Skavronskaya), by whom he had five sons and six daughters; the two eldest (Anna and Elizabeth) were legitimized by the marriage.

In 1721, by the decision of the Senate and the Holy Synod, Peter I adopted the title Peter the Great, Emperor and Father of the Fatherland.

Peter died in 1725 without designating an heir. The problem of succession arose because on February 5, 1722, he passed a law which disregarded the ancient principle of hereditary seniority and proclaimed instead that the sovereign could appoint his successor. This new law gave rise to a series of palace revolutions.

After Peter's death, his body was transferred to the Peter and Paul Cathedral where, placed in a specially designed sarcophagus, it remained until 1731, when it was committed to the earth.

# CATHERINE I.
## 1684–1727

Her real name was Martha Skavronskaya. Daughter of a Lithuanian peasant, born in 1684 in Ringen (Swedish province of Livonia), she received practically no education, and was instructed only in the rudiments of reading and housekeeping. For a brief span Catherine was the wife of a Swedish dragoon. At the beginning of the Great Northern War she was taken prisoner and installed in the domestic service of Field Marshal Boris Sheremetev. Then she was transferred to the household of Alexander Menshikov, a close friend and associate of Peter I. In 1705, she was privately married to Peter I. The marriage was formalized in 1712. Catherine possessed great vitality, was merry, good-natured and adaptable, and had an earthy common sense which helped her to soothe and cheer Peter and give him balance in moments of ungovernable rage or despondancy. In 1711, she accompanied Peter on the Pruth campaign where her clever advice helped rescue the Russian army when it was surrounded by the enemy. To commemorate her role in the Pruth campaign Peter created a new decoration, the Order of St. Catherine for Ladies, founded under the name of the Order of Deliverance.

In 1724, Catherine was crowned empress and in 1725, after Peter died without naming an heir, the issue of succession was quickly settled in favor of Catherine. But the real ruler of the state during Catherine's reign, which lasted only two years and three months, was Menshikov who headed the Supreme Privy Council. Catherine I died in 1727 and was laid to rest beside Peter I in the Peter and Paul Cathedral.

# PETER II.
## 1715–1730

Grandson of Peter I, son of Peter's eldest son Alexei and Princess Charlotte-Sophie of Brunswick-Wolfenbüttel. Born in 1715 in St. Petersburg, and orphaned in childhood (his mother died soon after his birth), he was left in the hands of Peter I and Catherine who treated him with negligence. The old nobility, the clergy and the people at large regarded the Tsarevich as the rightful heir, though before her death Catherine I had wished to leave the throne to one of her daughters. But the Supreme Privy Council in the presence of Guards officers decided in favor of Peter's grandson, who succeeded as Peter II in 1727 and was crowned in 1728. Peter II was only twelve when he ascended the throne, so he was controlled by the Supreme Privy Council who acted as regents. His brief reign was marked by the intrigues of various palace factions which, pursuing their own interests, entertained plans of marrying the young emperor to, by turns, Peter I's daughter Elizabeth, Peter's sister Natalia, Princess Maria Menshikova or Princess Ekaterina Dolgorukaya. But early in 1730, when Peter II was not quite fifteen years old, he died of smallpox without designating an heir. Peter II was buried in the Cathedral of the Archangel Michael in the Moscow Kremlin and with his death the male line of the Romanovs came to an end.

## ANNA IOANNOVNA. 1693–1740

Niece of Peter I, daughter of Peter I's elder half-brother Ioann Alexeyevich and Tsarina Praskovya Fedorovna. Born in 1693 in Moscow. Anna's childhood was unhappy: her passive and feeble father was alienated from all practical state and family affairs; Tsarina Praskovya neglected and even hated her daughters. Anna did not receive an education appropriate to her station. She knew a little German and could barely write in Russian. In 1710, Peter I married her to Friedrich Wilhelm, Duke of Courland, who died soon after the wedding. For nineteen years Anna lived at Mitau in Courland, visiting Russia only on rare occasions.

The unexpected death of Peter II decided Anna's fate: the Supreme Council offered her the Russian throne and in April 1730 she was crowned. Her ten-year reign was dominated by Ernst-Johann Biron, Duke of Courland, her favorite and First Minister in Courland.

Anna died in 1740 and was buried in the Peter and Paul Cathedral.

## ANNA LEOPOLDOVNA. 1718–1746

Née Elizabeth Catherine Christine, Princess of Mecklenburg-Schwerin, niece of Empress Anna Ioannovna, daughter of Anna's elder sister Ekaterina Ioannovna and Duke Karl-Leopold of Mecklenburg-Schwerin. Born in 1718 in Rostock. In 1722, she accompanied her mother to Russia where she stayed at the court of Anna Ioannovna. In 1733, she was received into the Orthodox Church and rechristened Anna in honor of the Empress. In 1739, Anna Ioannovna, married her to Anton Ulrich, Duke of Brunswick-Lüneburg, and appointed their newly-born son Ioann Antonovich her successor under the regency of Biron. In 1740, Anna Leopoldovna deposed Biron and assumed the regency during the minority of her son.

Ill-bred, careless and lazy, she showed little capacity for administration. Nevertheless she intended to proclaim herself empress but on the night of February 25, 1741, was overthrown by Elizabeth, daughter of Peter I, and arrested. She was confined at Kholmogory on the White Sea together with her husband and children born in exile, where she died in 1746. She was buried in the Alexander Nevsky Lavra in St. Petersburg.

## IVAN (IOANN) VI. 1740–1764

Son of Anna Leopoldovna and Anton Ulrich, Duke of Brunswick-Lüneburg. Born in 1740 in St. Petersburg. Shortly before her death Empress Anna Ioannovna had nominated him successor to the throne. At the age of fifteen months he was dethroned by Elizabeth, daughter of Peter I, who first intended to send him and his family abroad. From 1741 to 1744 Ivan was confined in the fortresses of Dünamünde and Ranenburg, then at Kholmogory, where he was kept isolated from his family. He remained there until 1756, before being moved to the Schlüsselburg fortress, where he remained in solitary confinement for eight years.

In 1764, Ivan was murdered by his guards to forestall an attempt to release him.

# ELIZABETH I (ELIZAVETA PETROVNA). 1709–1761

Daughter of Peter I and Catherine I. Born in 1709 in Moscow. Of all Peter's surviving descendants she was, by far, the most legitimate heir to the Russian throne. Regarding Elizabeth as a rival, Empress Anna Ioannovna and Anna Leopoldovna removed her from the court after the death of Catherine I. She lived in seclusion for fourteen years surrounded by her friends and supporters who opposed the German domination at the Russian court.

Elizabeth had secretly married Alexei Razumovsky, son of a Chernigov cossack, whom she elevated to the position of cantor in her private chapel, and when she became empress she conferred on him the title of count. A sociable and lively person who could wear men's clothes with flair, Elizabeth enjoyed great popularity in the army, especially the Guards regiments which helped her to seize the throne in 1741. She was crowned in 1742 and ruled for twenty years. The absence of an heir told on the stability of Elizabeth's position in the first years of her reign and, wishing to reaffirm herself in the eyes of Russian society, she summoned to Russia her nephew Karl Peter Ulrich from Holstein-Gottorp (the future Peter III).

Elizabeth died in 1761 and was buried in the Peter and Paul Cathedral next to Peter I and Catherine I.

# PETER III. 1728–1762

The only son of Karl Friedrich, Duke of Holstein-Gottorp, and Peter I's eldest daughter Anna, he was born in 1728 in Kiel, and was the grandson of both Peter I and his chief antagonist on the battlefield, King Charles XII of Sweden; he could thus lay claims equally to the crown of Russia and that of Sweden. During the reign of Catherine I his parents had renounced their rights to the Russian throne for themselves and their descendants. But in 1742, by the command of his aunt Elizabeth, he arrived in Russia and, having been admitted into the Orthodox Church under the name Peter Fedorovich, was declared her successor. In 1745, he married Princess Sophie Augusta Fredericka of Anhalt-Zerbst who was rechristened Catherine (the future Catherine II). They had two children, Anna and Paul (the future Emperor Paul I). Feeble, ill-bred, poorly educated and hating Russia, Peter caused Empress Elizabeth much anxiety during the last years of her reign. She even considered nominating Peter's son Paul or his wife Catherine as her successor. But, as she could not make up her mind, upon her death in 1761 Peter Fedorovich ascended the throne as Peter III.

During the 1762 palace revolution Peter III was forced to abdicate. He was removed to the Ropsha castle where, in July 6, 1762, he was assassinated by the conspirators headed by the Orlov brothers. Peter III was buried in the Alexander Nevsky Lavra in St. Petersburg and later reburied – by order of Paul I – in the Peter and Paul Cathedral beside Catherine II.

# CATHERINE II. 1729–1762

Née Princess Sophie Augusta Fredericka of Anhalt-Zerbst. Born in Stettin in 1729. When she was fourteen, Empress Elizabeth chose her as the wife of Peter Fedorovich. In 1744, in the company of her mother the young princess came to Russia where she was admitted into the Orthodox Church and adopted the name Ekaterina Alexeyevna. In 1745, she was married to Peter Fedorovich.

Seeing herself as the future autocrat of Russia, she made a point of studying the customs, language and way of life of the Russians and read avidly. After the death of Empress Elizabeth her position at the court of Peter III worsened and it was generally thought that she would be forced to take the veil.

Supported by the Guards, Catherine led the successful coup in midsummer 1762. On September 22, 1762, she was crowned as Empress Catherine II and ruled the state for thirty-four years. She died in 1796 and was buried in the Peter and Paul Cathedral.

# PAUL I.
## 1754–1801

Son of Peter III and Catherine II. Born in St. Petersburg in 1754. From the day of his birth Elizabeth removed Paul from his mother and looked after him herself. Later, after the deposition of Peter III and the accession of Catherine II to the throne, he was kept away from power by his mother. Paul lived in seclusion at Gatchina, near St. Petersburg, organizing his own army on the Prussian model and drawing up projects for administrative reforms.

In 1773, he married Princess Wilhelmine of Hesse-Darmstadt, rechristened Natalia Alexeyevna. After her death in 1776, he married Princess Sophie Dorothea of Württemberg rechristened Maria Fedorovna by whom he had four sons, Alexander (the future Alexander I), Konstantin, Nikolai (the future Nicholas I) and Mikhail, and seven daughters: Alexandra, Elena, Anna, Ekaterina, Maria, Elizaveta and Olga.

After the death of Catherine II in 1796, he ascended the throne and in 1797 was crowned as Paul I, Emperor of Russia. At the time of his coronation, he changed the law of succession to the Russian throne: primogeniture in the male line replaced Peter the Great's provision of free selection by the reigning monarch.

On the night of March 11, 1801 he was killed in a palace revolution. Buried in the Peter and Paul Cathedral.

# ALEXANDER I.
## 1777–1825

Eldest son of Paul I, born in St. Petersburg in 1777. His childhood and boyhood was marred by the animosity between his father, Paul, and his grandmother, Catherine II, who disliked her son and focused all her attention on Alexander's upbringing. At the court of his father, he was treated with distrust. According to recently found data, Alexander was involved in Paul's assassination. An intelligent, well-bred man with a talent for diplomacy and gentle manners, he lacked consistency and firmness of purpose and with the passage of time became more and more suspicious of people.

Upon his succession in 1801, Alexander declared that he would adhere faithfully to Catherine the Great's policies. The coronation ceremony took place on September 5, 1801. His wife Louise Augusta Marie, daughter of Prince Karl Ludwig of Baden, was rechristened Elizaveta Alexeyevna; she enjoyed popularity at the court for her kind disposition and friendliness but did not have much influence on affairs of state. Their children, daughters Elizaveta and Maria, died in infancy.

On November 18, 1825, Alexander I died unexpectedly at Taganrog where he had accompanied his consort for the sake of her health. Empress Elizaveta Alexeyevna died at Belev, Tula province, in 1826. They were buried in the Peter and Paul Cathedral.

# NICHOLAS I.
## 1796–1855

Third son of Paul I, born at Tsarskoye Selo near St. Petersburg in 1796. His education, unlike that of his brothers, Alexander and Konstantin, was focused mainly on the military arts. He was trained for a military career and had little acquaintance with governmental affairs. In 1817, he married Fredericka Louise Charlotte Wilhelmine, daughter of Friedrich Wilhelm III of Prussia, who was admitted into the Orthodox Church and adopted the name Alexandra Fedorovna. They had seven children: Alexander (the future Emperor Alexander II), Nikolai, Konstantin, Mikhail, Maria, Olga and Alexandra.

He ascended the throne in 1825 after the sudden death of Alexander I, who had no children, and the abdication on the part of the immediate heir Konstantin, Nicholas's elder brother, who was Governor-General of the Polish Kingdom. He was crowned in Moscow in 1826 and in Warsaw in 1829.

Nicholas I died in St. Petersburg in 1855. Empress Alexandra Fedorovna died in Tsarskoye Selo in 1860. They were buried in the Peter and Paul Cathedral.

# ALEXANDER II. 1818–1881

Eldest son of Nicholas I, born in Moscow in 1818. He received a solid military and general education as well as considerable practical training in the affairs of state. Alexander's teachers included the well-known lawyer and statesman Mikhail Speransky and the poet Vasily Zhukovsky. At the age of seven Alexander was proclaimed heir apparent. Coming of age, he began to take interest in matters of state administration. In 1837, he traveled extensively through Russia, and was the first member of the royal family to visit Siberia. In 1841, Alexander married Maximiliana Wilhelmine Augusta Sophie Marie, Princess of Hesse Darmstadt, who was rechristened Maria Alexandrovna. They had six sons: Nikolai, Alexander (the future Emperor Alexander III), Vladimir, Alexei, Sergei and Pavel, and two daughters Alexandra and Maria.

Alexander ascended the throne in 1855 and was crowned in 1856. Twelve attempts on his life were made by revolutionary populists. On March 1, 1881, when driving along the Catherine Canal near Nevsky Prospekt he was mortally wounded by a bomb. He was buried in the Peter and Paul Cathedral. Empress Maria Alexandrovna, who died on May 22, 1880, was also buried there.

# ALEXANDER III. 1845–1894

Second son of Alexander II, born in St. Petersburg in 1845. He received a general and military education under the guidance of professors from St. Petersburg and Moscow universities. Upon the death of his elder brother Nikolai in 1865, Alexander became heir to the Russian throne. In 1866, he married Princess Sophie Fredericka Dagmar, daughter of Christian IX of Denmark, who was admitted into the Orthodox Church as Maria Fedorovna. They had four sons, Nikolai (the future Emperor Nicholas II), Georgi, Mikhail and Alexander, and two daughters, Xenia and Olga.

Alexander ascended the throne in 1881. After his father's assassination, fearing new attacks, he secluded himself for some time in his palace at Gatchina (which earned him the nickname "Prisoner of Gatchina"). His coronation took place in 1883.

In 1894, Alexander III died prematurely at Livadia in the Crimea, and was buried in the Peter and Paul Cathedral.

Empress Maria Fedorovna left Russia in 1918 after the October Revolution. She died in Denmark in 1929.

# NICHOLAS II. 1868–1918

Eldest son of Alexander III, born at Tsarskoye Selo near St. Petersburg. He received a private education, focused mainly on the study of law, economics and military arts. As the heir to the throne he took part in the work of the State Council and the Cabinet of Ministers. In 1894, he was betrothed to Princess Alix of Hesse, daughter of Grand Duke Ludwig of Hesse and Princess Alice of Great Britain and granddaughter of Queen Victoria. She came to Russia shortly before Alexander III's death and was admitted into the Orthodox Church as Alexandra Fedorovna. Their wedding took place on February 14, 1894. They had five children: a single son Alexis, heir apparent, and daughters Olga, Anastasia, Tatyana, and Maria.

Nicholas II ascended the throne in 1894 and was crowned on May 14, 1896. There was a palace coup brewing to depose Nicholas II, but after the events of the February revolution on March 2, 1917, the Emperor abdicated at Pskov for himself and his son in favor of his brother, Grand Duke Mikhail, who in turn abdicated the next day.

On March 8, 1917, the Provisional Government placed the Imperial family under arrest at Tsarskoye Selo, then they were moved to Tobolsk in Siberia, from where they were transferred to Ekaterinburg. There, on the night of July 16 1918, the Tsar and his family were cruelly murdered by the Bolsheviks. Nicholas II has been canonized as the "Holy Most Orthodox Martyr Nicholas."